Improving Instructional Practice

Other Books by Wafa Hozien

SLLA Crash Course: Approaches for Success (Rowman & Littlefield, January 2017)
Leading the Next Generation: Case Studies for Elementary School Principals (2018)
Reflective Practice: Case Studies for High School Principals (2018)

Improving Instructional Practice

*Resolving Issues in
Leadership through Case Studies*

Wafa Hozien

ROWMAN & LITTLEFIELD
Lanham • Boulder • New York • London

Published by Rowman & Littlefield
A wholly owned subsidiary of The Rowman & Littlefield Publishing Group, Inc.
4501 Forbes Boulevard, Suite 200, Lanham, Maryland 20706
www.rowman.com

Unit A, Whitacre Mews, 26-34 Stannary Street, London SE11 4AB, United Kingdom

Copyright © 2017 by Wafa Hozien

All rights reserved. No part of this book may be reproduced in any form or by any electronic or mechanical means, including information storage and retrieval systems, without written permission from the publisher, except by a reviewer who may quote passages in a review.

British Library Cataloguing in Publication Information Available

Library of Congress Cataloging-in-Publication Data

Includes bibliographic references.
978-1-4758-3643-1 (cloth : alk. paper)
978-1-4758-3644-8 (pbk. : alk. paper)
978-1-4758-3645-5 (electronic)

∞ ™ The paper used in this publication meets the minimum requirements of American National Standard for Information Sciences Permanence of Paper for Printed Library Materials, ANSI/NISO Z39.48-1992.

Printed in the United States of America

For my mother, Zakieh Hozien, who believed in me
and taught me my work ethic.
For my father, Ismail Hozien, who was patient and kind.

Contents

Foreword ix

Introduction xiii

1 Assessing Student Learning 1
2 Classroom Management 13
3 Distinctive Student Abilities 29
4 Teaching and Learning 51
5 Technology Matters 73

Selected Bibliography 105
About the Author 111

Foreword

Wafa Hozien has written an excellent resource and training tool for emergent or experienced teacher leaders. In recent years, many who research and analyze educational best practices have focused on the teacher as the key variable related to students' academic success. This is true, no doubt, but also an incomplete conclusion. Michael Fullan, an internationally regarded authority on school system change, has rightly taken this view to a more nuanced level. He sees the school principal as a key driver of teacher success through effective leadership of cultural change. But he notes that the foundation of education is the teacher: it is from teacher ranks that future school administrators are developed and promoted. Dr. Hozien recognizes this view in the book of case studies she has created, as they are designed to develop instructional leaders among the teacher corps who will become the successful school administrators to lead and sustain Fullan's important prescription for cultural change.

Today's schools are complex political entities. Those who work there confront pressure from all engaged parties: parents want each child to have an excellent personalized learning environment that gives their child a competitive edge; students must be inspired and prepared for the next step in their lives; local leaders expect the schools to be an economic driver that will attract businesses to the community. These demands require a high level of engagement from educators who are increasingly confronting classrooms full of diverse learners whose success will depend on their instructors' preparation, energy, and openness to continuous learning.

Public education in the United States has been found wanting in national and international evaluations of student achievement. If the United States is to keep its competitive edge, we educators must meet the expectations of our stakeholders. We must succeed at this important work in spite of increasing poverty among our young learners, decreasing resources and accountability systems that are not usually aligned to the outcomes students and parents seek.

These forces of change in public education have been increasing over time. When you add into the mixture resource cutbacks and a new generation of teachers and leaders who have had less preparation in both their pre-service and in-service training time, we confront the potential for decline. This situation will be even made more dire if competition for resources shortchanges schools and instructional time is spent on tasks not congruent to desired outcomes. In the last twenty years competitive pressure from political sources has been added. The solution most often talked about is to increase the number and type of schools. Making more of something—schools—doesn't usually make them better. This is especially true when there is a smaller group of experienced and well-trained teachers and leaders to staff the new schools.

Fullan sees the key as the development of instructional leaders who are committed to improving teachers' working conditions and morale, but who also have the skills to develop and motivate toward a compelling vision and higher performance standards. We have long known from research that leader skills and behaviors have a great impact on teacher effectiveness and school climate. Effective teachers and a positive, inclusive school climate improve student outcomes and engagement. In fact some studies estimate a very high percentage of student outcomes can be attributed to teacher and leader behavior.

From my thirty-five years as superintendent of schools, I know this to be a fact. In the end, learning is a people-centered activity. Relationships matter. At the center of a successful school or school system is a climate that is conducive to learning. I believe this occurs through a values-driven, hands-on management style that supports a positive and productive workplace. This management style can be learned and developed from within through contextual education and the modeling of effective leader behavior.

Here is where Dr. Hozien's case study book is of tremendous value. By increasing the quality and effectiveness of leader training we can improve both the climate and outcomes for students. These case studies are insightful, understandable, easy to read, provoke thoughtful discussions, and offer an opportunity to learn in context in a manner that is accessible to educators whose confront a dearth of professional development opportunities. This case study format is user friendly and addresses everyday instructional situations and challenges. Many of the studies illustrate not only the who, what, when, and why, of the issue that presents itself for resolution, but how it feels to the teacher, learner, and leader.

Michael Fullan has organized a framework around three major domains: human capital, social capital and decisional capital. His premise is that these domains serve as the foundation for a school or entire school system's pedagogical transformation. These case studies would be congruent with this framework. The case studies are useful in training emergent leaders in preparation for the assistant principal or principal roles. They also are beneficial to teacher leaders and small instructional groups. The case studies—particularly if employed as a group learning opportunity—can create clarity and a shared understanding of the factors that affect resolution of issues common in the classroom and school building. Case studies that develop questions, alternatives, and possible solutions for discussion also enhance engagement and changes in behavior. I highly recommend this well-constructed resource to any group or individual involved in training the next generation of leaders in public education.

—Jerry D. Weast

Jerry D. Weast*, EdD, founder and CEO of the Partnership for Deliberate Excellence, LLC, is a national consultant to foundations and organizations working to improve public schools. His more than forty years in public education include thirty-five years as a school system superintendent. He led Montgomery County (Maryland) Public Schools to national recognition for its focus on equity and excellence, leading to student success across all socioeconomic groups.*

Introduction

IN THE HEARTLAND OF SERVICE

Most school administrators serve their school communities more than eighty hours a week and therefore are at the cusp of the latest teaching and learning practices. Some school principals consistently use innovative practices to increase student achievement, therefore being at the heart of increasing student outcomes. This book is about how the present or future school administrator will be improving instructional leadership behaviors, practices, or actions. This involves knowing and understanding what effective instructional leadership looks like. We all know that it focuses on the student and learning. Now the challenge is to implement effective instructional leadership strategies, and that is where this book comes in. But as a future school leader, you have to be willing to look in the mirror and make the necessary changes leading to improved instructional practices. By resolving the case studies provided for you in this book, they should help you toward improving instructional leadership. This book constitutes a collection of case studies that explore issues faced by administrators in instructional school settings, with the scenarios designed to develop the Professional Standards for Educational Leaders.

Instructional leadership is at the heart of what school administrators do. It has been defined as a moral responsibility in which school leaders are thoroughly committed to both the success of students and the growth of teachers; therefore, when individuals consider moving into administration, they must do so with the understanding that their personal performance can help mediocre teachers develop into average teachers, or average teachers grow into outstanding teachers (Robbins and Alvy, 2004).

With ample evidence suggesting that the quality of instruction is paramount to student achievement (Marzano, 2006; Reeves, 2004, 2006, 2011; Schmoker, 2006) and principals in turn seeking to promote instructional improvement in their schools (Glickman, Gordon, and Ross-Gordon, 2010; Marzano, Frontier, and Livingston, 2011), the purpose of this book is to understand the thinking and practice of school principals who will be leading with a focus on their development and for instructional improvement and focusing on teaching and learning at the core of schooling. The focus of this book is to keep schooling focused on that instructional core, that is, students and teachers in the presence of content.

Teachers and school principals are the focus here with the interviews and observations of the formal observation cycle (pre-observation conference, observation, post-observation conference) helping the reader gain insight into how school principals differentiate their instructional leadership by devising and implementing different supports and challenges for teachers with varied developmental needs and orientations.

Additionally, by analyzing these case studies, school leaders can better understand their approach and beliefs about instructional leadership. By working through the resolution of these case studies, the student can actively implement a "leadership model" that they work through and have differentiated modes of feedback and attend to differences in teachers' ways of knowing. While these case studies alone are not sufficient to guarantee instructional improvement, they do support teachers from a range of developmental orientations to achieve instructional success. Still, school principals felt most comfortable supporting teachers who shared their particular vision of schooling.

For many reasons associated with their own knowledge, skill, developmental orientations, and unique school contexts, school principals will struggle, albeit for different reasons, to lead optimally at the nexus of instructional improvement. With analysis of these case studies at the core of improved instructional leadership practices, the reader should be able to identify and implement concrete strategies, specifically when treating the formal observation cycle as collegial inquiry, to employ an ever-evolving instructional leadership model with professional growth at its core, an approach to leadership that connects development with a clear vision and framework for instructional improvement. Therefore, with these case studies the reader will uncover the transformative possibilities when school leaders, and indeed leaders across disciplines, invest time in the process of their own development in service of supporting others.

Every person who has sat in a public school classroom recognizes the transformative power of an effective teacher. We can name the teachers who were good and which ones were very bad; the names of the ones who just did not have any impact on lives fade away over time.

What we know is that high-performing and effective teachers can help guide their students to success whether their goal is higher education or a vocation. Empirically, it is known that these effective teachers can have a direct influence in enhancing student learning (Baker et al., 2010; Darling-Hammond, 2000; Stronge and Tucker, 2003; Taylor and Tyler, 2012). To improve education in America, school leaders are challenged to support and cultivate effective teachers in our schools so that all children have the opportunity to reach their fullest potential. This book explores how principals in school settings can improve how their school's teaching practices, using a framework of improving teaching, might address these challenges and help school administrators improve their instructional practices. This framework is designed to support student achievement and professional best practices through increased dialogue, classroom understandings, instruction, and professionalism. The cases presented here explore a myriad of topics including social media and gender orientation—topics highly relevant in today's ever changing society.

SECTION I. OVERVIEW OF INSTRUCTIONAL LEADERSHIP

To be considered an effective instructional leader, according to the National Association of Elementary School Principals (2008), principals need to follow six roles: make student and adult learning the priority, set high expectations for performance, gear content and instruction to standards, create a culture of continuous learning for adults, use multiple sources of data to assess learning, and activate the community's support for school success. A seventh and eighth role is to engage teachers in instructional dialogue and evaluate classroom practices (Glanz, 2003).

In their research of instructional leadership practices perceived to be beneficial to teachers, Blase and Blase (2000) identified seven behaviors successful instructional leaders exhibit:

- Making suggestions
- Giving feedback
- Soliciting opinions
- Modeling effective instruction
- Supporting collaboration
- Providing professional development opportunities
- Giving praise for effective teaching

Though the instructional leadership approach is the current model of choice, there are some who claim the role of principal is far too big for one person to handle alone. Most building level administrators' days are filled with managerial activities leaving very little time to focus on the genuine instructional leadership of analyzing teaching practices, providing instructional guidance, and monitoring the curriculum (Fink and Resnick, 2001). Lloyd, Robinson, and Rowe (2008) pointed out that the flaw with the instructional leadership approach is that building leaders are often not adequately qualified to be the instructional expert in the building.

Administrative preparation programs have not adequately prepared principals to take on the additional role of instructional leadership (Bowers, Marks, and Printy, in press). Fullan (2002) contended, "The role of the principal as instructional leader is too narrow a concept to carry the weight of the kinds of reforms that will create the schools that we need for the future" (p. 17).

Conclusion

It is important to understand the role of the impactful instructional school leader. This book is relevant for school leaders contemplating how best to support, design, develop, and implement an effective teacher evaluation system. This book can help districts transform the teacher evaluation process from merely an exercise in state compliance into a tool that can link effective teacher evaluation to improved teacher practices.

The role of the principal is complicated and ever-changing (Sergiovanni, 2001). Traditionally, the school community perceived the principal as a father figure, and he was judged by how well he managed day-to-day operations. In the past twenty-five years or so, the expectations have shifted. Principals are expected to be visionaries (Bolman and Deal, 2003), systems managers and thinkers (Hallinger, 1992; Heifetz and Linsky, 2002; Sergiovanni, 2001), transformational leaders (Leithwood, 1994; Marks and Printy, 2003; Marzano, Waters, and McNulty, 2005), and now even instructional leaders (Hallinger, 1992; Marks and Printy, 2003; Marzano, Waters, and McNulty, 2005). Although the role prescription of the principal has changed over time, the constant has been that the principal is responsible for almost everything that occurs in a building, including the quality of instruction. This book is meant to regenerate dialogue on effective teaching and learning practices and how to enhance them.

For the field as a whole, my hope is that the book provides not only practical guidance of school leader and practice but to add needed complexity and nuance to ongoing conversations on how to prepare students for college and career. Though the Common Core and whatever is coming down the pipeline in the form of assessment is no more than a set of end-of-year articulations of what students need to know and be able to do, it has mistakenly been perceived as an initiative, a curriculum, and/or a professional development focus, the result of which has been hundreds of millions of dollars spent by states, districts, and schools on training and resources that have not met teachers' needs (Kaufman et al., 2016) and appear to have had minimal impact on student achievement (Loveless, 2016). The real impact is on teaching and learning and in instructional leadership.

SECTION II: HOW TO USE THIS BOOK

Analyzing the Cases

This is how each of the case studies can be used in class. Read the case prior to class discussion. You will learn very little from others' presentations or discussion if you have not familiarized yourself with the material and issues involved in the case. Get in groups of two or more, depending on class size, and fill in the worksheet at the end of this section, keeping in mind the teacher evaluation tool to be combined with the case study analysis. One person records the actual conversation onto the worksheet, then another person presents the findings to the entire class. This can be done in an online setting as well, as Blackboard allows you to create groups and then come back together as a class. Or the instructor can opt to have one student work on one case study and then present to the online class.

Read the case initially to familiarize yourself with its basic content and issues under discussion. What is the case all about? What are the instructional issues highlighted? It might then be a good idea to examine the questions set by your instructor and reread the case thoroughly with these questions in mind, maybe using a highlighter pen as you reread in light of the task. In doing this, you should hopefully be able to identify how the tools and frameworks of strategic management could be used to answer the questions set. It might be useful to read any set questions prior to you rereading the case, as these can often give you a feel for the type of strategic issues the case may be addressing.

You might feel you have inadequate information in a particular case. This is real life. It is unlikely that a school principal will ever have all of the information s/he requires to make a decision. It is practice, therefore, in case analysis to make reasonable assumptions but explicitly state why you feel it is a reasonable assumption to make. In summary:

- Read the case before the class.
- Read the case questions to understand the strategic issues you are expected to address.
- Make sure you understand any data explained.
- Make sure you explain the rationale for any assumptions made in your analysis.

- Draw conclusions from issues identified.

Guidelines for Using Case Studies in Class

Strategy tools allow you to better understand the different specific instructional issues in different situations and contexts. Using these tools will allow you the opportunity to demonstrate to your class that you fully understand the rationale of applying skill sets, which skill sets can be applied in different cases, and the limitations of some of the skills you have acquired in your principal preparation program in certain school contexts.

A framework one could use is the school district teacher observation model, value-added analysis, evaluation of a teacher's choice of strategy, identification of what the key implementation issues are, and how might problems of implementation be addressed; this might require you to apply the cultural context, due to the fact that the setting is rural, urban, or suburban, and the like, or contextual analysis. The issues being addressed in the case should become clear as you read and reread the entire case or parts of the case through several times (Christensen, 1981).

Depending on the course objectives, the instructor may encourage students to follow a systematic approach to their analysis. Here is one way to approach the case studies in this book:

Steps in Analyzing a Case Study

1. Identify the problem(s) posited by the case.
2. Analyze: Think through this material and justify why you have reached your conclusions.
3. Decide/decision making: Identify a specific course of action for a school.
4. Application: Demonstrate your understanding.
5. Communication: Justify your decisions, course of action, and so on.

Usually students will work in groups in analyzing cases. This enhances their social skills through discussion, debate, and compromise. These are important skills in the world of work, where many people work on projects or set tasks as part of a team. Students might be expected to use case analysis as part of an assessment for school leaders. Students must therefore be able to summarize information succinctly and identify the most important points in the case, rather than merely regurgitating the case word for word (Schweitzer, 2014).

In the most straightforward application, the presentation of the case study establishes a framework for analysis. It is helpful if the statement of the case provides enough information for the students to figure out solutions and then to identify how to apply those solutions in other similar situations. Instructors may choose to use several cases so that students can identify both the similarities and differences among the cases.

For each case study in this book, try to understand how to resolve the instructional leadership issue. This can be done by answering the questions at the end of each case study, or you can create a worksheet that looks like the one below for all the case studies, thereby creating a systematic analysis of the case studies.

Depending on the course objectives, the instructor may encourage students to follow a systematic approach to their analysis. Here is another example:

PROFESSIONAL STANDARDS FOR EDUCATION LEADERS IN 2015

A key component of this book is that all of the case studies are aligned with the Interstate School Leaders Licensure Consortium standards. The ISSLC practice/policy standards were replaced by Professional Standards for Educational Leaders (PSEL) as national standards in November 2015. These are standards approved by the National Policy Board for Education Administration (2015) geared toward all educational stakeholders. The case studies focus on the following:

Standard 1. Mission, Vision, and Core Values: Effective educational leaders develop, advocate, and enact a shared mission, vision, and core values of high-quality education and academic success and well-being of each student.

Standard 2. Ethics and Professional Norms: Effective educational leaders act ethically and according to professional norms to promote each student's academic success and well-being.

Standard 3. Equity and Cultural Responsiveness: Effective educational leaders strive for equity of educational opportunity and culturally responsive practices to promote each student's academic success and well-being.

Standard 4. Curriculum, Instruction, and Assessment: Effective educational leaders develop and support intellectually rigorous and coherent systems of curriculum, instruction, and assessment to promote each student's academic success and well-being.

Standard 5. Community of Care and Support for Students: Effective educational leaders cultivate an inclusive, caring, and supportive school community that promotes the academic success and well-being of each student.

Standard 6. Professional Capacity of School Personnel: Effective educational leaders develop the professional capacity and practice of school personnel to promote each student's academic success and well-being.

Standard 7. Professional Community for Teachers and Staff: Effective educational leaders foster a professional community of teachers and other professional staff to promote each student's academic success and well-being.

Standard 8. Meaningful Engagement of Families and Community: Effective educational leaders engage families and the community in meaningful, reciprocal, and mutually beneficial ways to promote each student's academic success and well-being.

Standard 9. Operations and Management: Effective educational leaders manage school operations and resources to promote each student's academic success and well-being.

Standard 10. School Improvement: Effective educational leaders act as agents of continuous improvement to promote each student's academic success and well-being.

Case Study Analysis Table 1

Case Study Title
What issues are at stake here?
What should the principal do? (probe for why/justification)
If necessary, create a step-by-step short-term/long-term action plan
What would you hope your action/decision would accomplish?
What possible risks or "downsides" are there to your action/decision?

Table by author.

Chapter One

Assessing Student Learning

CASE STUDY 1.1
CHECKING FOR UNDERSTANDING

Standards 3.b and 4.f

Topic: Middle School. The school principal works with faculty to address concerns over the achievement scores at Rosa Parks Middle School. This is a case about Formative Assessment.

The sun shone brightly down on Rosa Parks Middle School one morning in October as students arrived on their buses and made their way into the building. Mr. Harrow, the principal, greeted students as they passed him near the doorway. He asked them if they had their homework or if they were ready for the day, but he also asked them about their families. "Is grandma better now that she is out of the hospital?" Mr. Harrow had grown up in the neighborhood and had been the principal of Parks Middle for fifteen years. He knew the students and the community, and the students knew he was a face they could count on.

Parks Middle served 1,600 students in grades six through eight. The student body is diverse, coming from the surrounding urban neighborhoods in an older part of the city. Eighty percent of the students were minority, and 85 percent of the students qualified for free or reduced lunch. Mr. Harrow knew the challenges that the student body faced and that they presented to the teaching faculty. Over his fifteen-year tenure, the staff at Parks had received cultural competency training, training in classroom management strategies, and training in differentiation strategies.

The school had also implemented a system of Positive Behavior Interventions and Supports, and students had responded well to the consistent expectations and the system of rewards and consequences in each classroom. Test scores and student achievement had increased at Parks Middle, but Mr. Harrow still was not satisfied. The school still had scores below the state average, and Mr. Harrow knew his students could do better.

Over the past three years, Mr. Harrow had been leading the staff through a study of student achievement scores and a discussion of the root causes. The staff had studied high-impact strategies, using John Hattie's Visible Learning to identify strategies that they could implement that were proven effective in raising student achievement scores. The faculty had settled on implementing a stronger system of formative assessments. Teachers agreed that they needed more checks for understanding along the way so that they could immediately address misconceptions or gaps in student learning by remediating and reviewing during instruction instead of waiting to review and try to fill gaps just before the assessments.

Last spring, the teachers at Parks Middle had begun to infuse more formative assessments in their lesson plans, and this fall the teachers were fully implementing the formative assessments. Teachers were expected to have at least two checks for understanding during each lesson, and a "ticket out the door" activity at the end of the class that asked students to sum up the day's learning. The checks for understanding could be verbal or written, but the ticket out the door had to be written, so that the teacher could use that information to inform instructional planning for the next day.

As the bell rang and students cleared from the hallways, Mr. Harrow made his way to Mrs. Gant's math classroom. Students were settling in when he arrived—getting out their notebooks, turning in the night's homework, and sharpening pencils. Mrs. Gant greeted each student as he or she entered the classroom, taking a few extra moments to encourage some that Mr. Harrow recognized as more in need of attention due to circumstances at home or due to behavior issues at school. After a few moments, the pledge and morning announcements were broadcast over the intercom, and then Mrs. Gant addressed the students. The class had spent the day before learning about how to solve for an unknown length of a side of a triangle. Mrs. Gant referenced the previous day's ticket out the door: "You all are still struggling with applying the formula when the triangle is not a right triangle. So, let's go over that information again. Can you look back in your notes and find the part where we talked about triangles that are not right triangles?"

Mrs. Gant waited a few moments for the students to find the correct information in their notes, and then she began to review the concept. Mr. Harrow took notes of his own, but he also looked at the notes of a student next to him to see what the student had recorded yesterday. Mrs. Gant's explanation today matched the notes from yesterday. After re-explaining, she demonstrated by showing an example on the board. She asked the students to copy her example into their notebooks.

"Now let's check for understanding," Mrs. Gant said. She drew another triangle on the board, labeling two sides and the height of the triangle. "Work this problem on your own to find the length of the third side," she instructed. The students diligently worked on the problem, and as they finished, they raised their hands for Mrs. Gant to look at their work. Mr. Harrow took notes of how Mrs. Gant interacted with students and responded to them individually. She quietly redirected a few students who did not begin the task when asked.

She did so by encouraging them to get started and reminded them to use their notes if they needed help. She praised two students who got the problem correct on the first attempt, and she encouraged students who did not have the right answer to continue trying. Mr. Harrow made a tally of the number of students who solved the problem correctly during the check for understanding and the number who did not. Four students solved the problem correctly; twenty-one students did not.

After looking at every student's paper, Mrs. Gant went back to the board and asked the students to direct their attention to her. She worked her way through the problem, explaining each step along the way. She asked the students to look at their own work and figure out where they made the mistake. When she was finished, she said, "See, that's how it's done! Do you understand it now?" The students nodded or said "yes." Mrs. Gant then moved on to the next part of the lesson.

Back in his office, Mr. Harrow reflected on what he had seen in the classroom. Mrs. Gant had bought in to the formative assessment strategies, and Mr. Harrow was proud of that. Previously, Mrs. Gant had used few formative strategies in the classroom, giving a quiz each Friday over the section of the math chapter and a test each month. Her daily instruction had included notes and practice problems. Students could ask her to work the problems that they struggled with on the homework, but many students at Parks Middle did not even complete the homework, so most of the time, Mrs. Gant was asked to work very few problems.

When Mrs. Gant came to see Mr. Harrow for the post-observation conference after the school day, Mr. Harrow began by praising her for implementing the formative assessment strategies. He asked her about the day's ticket out the door. Mrs. Gant frowned. "Well, I asked them to work a problem similar to the one that we worked while you were there. When I looked at them, though, most of the students still don't know how to do it. The formative assessment doesn't seem to be working. I have explained this now two different times—yesterday and today—and the students still don't know how to solve it."

Mr. Harrow smiled and said that the formative assessment was working exactly the way that it should. It had given Mrs. Gant information that she could use to plan instruction for the following day. He elaborated: "You have explained it two times, and they still do not understand. It's not that the formative assessment isn't working—it's that the students are not responding to the instruction. I noticed today that your explanation was very similar to the explanation from the day before. I also noticed that you worked a practice problem today, and you worked a practice problem the day before. The instruction was the same, but some students do not understand the concept based on the instruction."

Mrs. Gant looked thoughtful. "So, I need to instruct differently? I am not sure how to do that because the instruction is this—here's the formula, here's how you apply it, and there you go."

Mr. Harrow laughed. "It may be that simple to you, but it's not that simple to the students. Yes, the concept doesn't change—you may not teach them a different way to do it. However, can you go about teaching the concept in a different way? One of the things that we have learned in our professional development is that students respond when concepts are concrete and visible. Is there any way that you can make this concept more concrete and hands on for the students?"

Mrs. Gant thought for a minute and then mentioned a bucket of foam triangles of different shapes and sizes that she had been given by a fellow teacher. "I guess I could do an activity with them where we find the perimeter of those foam triangles."

Mr. Harrow nodded. "Another thing we have learned is that students have to be actively engaged in the learning. Is there any way that you can involve the students more in explaining their thinking as you go through examples and the checks for understanding?"

Mrs. Gant nodded again. "Instead of working the problem myself, I can ask students to work the problem and explain the steps."

Mr. Harrow agreed. "I also think it would be helpful for you to have students who are working out the problem incorrectly explain their thinking. This will give you more information about why they are making the mistakes that they are making." Mrs. Gant agreed to do this as well.

A week later, Mrs. Gant stopped by to see Mr. Harrow as he was preparing to go home for the day. "Mr. Harrow, I want to let you know that you were right. This formative assessment thing works just like it should. I have been trying some of the things that we talked about—letting the students work the problems and talk about their thinking and why they are doing what they are doing. Now, instead of having two checks for understanding, I feel like we are constantly having checks for understanding. I am learning so much about how the students think, and I am able to adjust and reteach immediately."

Questions for Discussion

a. How does Mr. Harrow work with his faculty to address his concerns over the achievement scores at Rosa Parks Middle School?
b. Mr. Harrow and his faculty choose to research strategies that have been shown to impact student achievement before deciding what to implement. Why would this be an important step for an administrator and faculty to take?
c. What does Mrs. Gant do well during her observation? What are her weaknesses?
d. Why does having the students work the problems and explain their math thinking work for Mrs. Gant?
e. Explain Mr. Harrow's assertion that the formative assessment worked exactly the way it should. How can this be true when most of the students got the answer wrong?
f. What other suggestions would you make for Mrs. Gant? What else can Mr. Harrow, as her administrator, do to help her grow as a teacher?

CASE STUDY 1.2
COACHING UP A VETERAN

Standards 4.c and 4.f

Topic: High School. This is about a coach teaching to the high school social studies state test. The principal goes through effective Instructional Strategies with a veteran teacher.

Mrs. Sanders finished checking her emails with a frown. She had been the principal of Torrance High School for less than a month, and she had already heard a lot about Coach Morgan. Coach Jeff Morgan had been coaching football and teaching social studies at Torrance for twenty years. In fact, he graduated from Torrance as a football star, attended college, and then settled back in his hometown. The rural, close-knit community treated him like a hero. Many people had either played football with him or for him, or knew his family, which had been a part of the community for several generations. Quite a bit of what Mrs. Sanders had heard as the new principal at Torrance was about Coach Morgan—the legend.

However, not everyone shared a favorable opinion of Coach Morgan, especially the parents of some of the students in his classes. Torrance High School served 1,200 students, and Coach Morgan was one of the US history teachers. He had been teaching US history for all of his twenty years at Torrance, as the previous administrations allowed him to continue in a subject he was familiar with so that he wouldn't have to "learn something new" while also "dedicating time to football." At least, this is what Coach Morgan had expressed to Mrs. Sanders when she spoke with him about taking on a civics and government course.

Even with those twenty years of experience teaching US history, Coach Morgan had still generated several parent complaints about the grades of students in the course. Just this morning, Mrs. Sanders had received an email from the parent of Hope Ryder, one of the top students in the junior class. Mr. Ryder had expressed his dissatisfaction with the US history course, claiming that all Hope did was take notes straight from the textbook and then take a test that came directly from those notes. He lamented that Hope wasn't really learning anything—except to memorize her notes.

Mrs. Sanders left her office and headed for Coach Morgan's room. She had received at least one parent complaint about the US history course each week of the school year so far. Coach Morgan always promised her he would take care of it, but Mrs. Sanders was starting to notice a pattern. As Mrs. Sanders entered the room, she realized that there was no question that Coach Morgan was involved in Torrance football. The walls were decorated with red and gray posters and pictures of past teams. Coach Morgan's bookshelf was lined with plaques and trophies, and even the bulletin board displayed newspaper clippings about football. Mrs. Sanders also noticed the stark whiteness of the whiteboard. The date was written in the top left corner, but no other information appeared on the board.

Mrs. Sanders took a seat near the back of the room and opened her notepad to take notes. The thirty students in the class were furiously writing down notes that were displayed on the overhead projector. These notes were typewritten, and Mrs. Sanders realized that they were typed onto overhead overlays—similar to the ones that she had used when still a classroom teacher in the late 1990s. The notes, it appeared, were the same ones that Coach Morgan had used for many years, and there were places where the black typeface had worn off of the notes—Coach Morgan had filled in the spaces with a dry erase marker.

As students took notes, Coach Morgan was providing commentary on the notes, but Mrs. Sanders noticed that he first read from the notes and then just provided a slightly more in-depth explanation or comment. Mrs. Sanders did not notice a lesson plan book, and there was no agenda on the board. The notes were focused on the Civil War. Mrs. Sanders briefly wondered about the pacing of instruction—four weeks into the course on US history, the students were learning about the Civil War—but a shift in Coach Morgan's voice caught her attention.

The students had come to the place in the notes where the Civil War began with the battle at Fort Sumter. Coach Morgan's voice had taken on an excited quality. He began to tell the students about a visit he had made to Fort Sumter and what he saw. He described taking a boat from a location near Charleston, South Carolina, out to the fort and being able to walk around the ruins of the fort. He talked with the students about the cannons he had seen and about the area around Charleston. Coach Morgan spent the remainder of the class period telling stories about his visit to Fort Sumter and to Charleston, South Carolina. Mrs. Sanders observed some students listening intently, but other students shifted their attention when they were no longer taking notes. Three students checked their cell phones—hiding them in their laps so Coach Morgan could not see. Two students were observed completing assignments for another class.

When the bell rang, the students closed their notebooks and moved to leave. Coach Morgan spoke to a few of the football players about practice or the week's game, but many of the students left the room without interacting with him. Coach Morgan walked back to speak with Mrs. Sanders.

Coach Morgan told Mrs. Sanders that he didn't get very far in the lesson and that he would have to catch up tomorrow. Mrs. Sanders expressed surprise at how quickly the class had gotten to the Civil War—four weeks into the course. Coach Morgan laughed and said he spent less time on the things that weren't as interesting to him or the students. So, after the American Revolution, he usually skipped ahead to the Civil War. As other students began to move into the classroom, Mrs. Sanders stood to leave and asked Coach Morgan to come and see her about the observation on the following day.

That evening, Mrs. Sanders reviewed assessment data for Coach Morgan. She noticed that the scores of his students on the state assessments were lower than those of the other teachers at Torrance. Mrs. Sanders also reviewed the US history standards for the course that Coach Morgan was teaching, and she recognized a disconnect. Many standards of the course related to the time period between the American Revolution and the Civil War. In fact, when Mrs. Sanders reviewed the pacing guide for the course, she saw that the Civil War was not supposed to be covered until December. This is important because the state high school assessments are coming up and the students needed to have all of the content covered by the date of the state exam.

Coach Morgan was scheduled to see Mrs. Sanders during his planning period the next day. Prior to the meeting, Mrs. Sanders thought very carefully about how she would address the issues she had seen in Coach Morgan's classroom. She knew that as a long-standing member of the Torrance faculty, Coach Morgan might not react to criticism well. She also knew that as the new face in the school, how she dealt with this situation could make or break her with the faculty and community at Torrance. She owed it to the students, however, to make sure she addressed the issues she had noticed.

Mrs. Sanders began the meeting with Coach Morgan by stating that she just wanted to have a conversation to get to know him a little better. She asked him about football: in the twenty years that he had been coaching football, what changes had he seen, was he still using the same playbook, did he have to change tactics depending on the different teams? Coach Morgan warmed to the conversation, explaining that the coaching staff reviewed the playbook every year, discussed the new opponents, discussed the makeup of their own team, and developed a strategy for each team and each season. While there might be some things that remained the same, to win games, he had to really study his team and the other teams and be willing to constantly change. Mrs. Sanders continued—how often did the team get new equipment or new uniforms, what advances had there been in safety equipment in his tenure? Coach Morgan spoke of the new uniforms each year, and the new safety features in equipment, especially with helmets.

Then, Mrs. Sanders shifted gears. She asked about the US history classroom. In the twenty years that Coach Morgan had been teaching US history, what changes had he seen in the curriculum standards, and was he still using the same lessons? Did he change his tactics depending on the different students in his classroom? Coach Morgan's eyes widened, and he suddenly looked down. Mrs. Sanders continued—how often did he try new equipment in his classroom—new technologies like the interactive white board or having kids access information online. Coach Morgan looked up at Mrs. Sanders and told her that he got her point? He smiled broadly.

Coach Morgan related to Mrs. Sanders that in his twenty years as a teacher and coach, football had been the number one priority. He felt that the administration was always happy with him as long as the football season was going well, and no one had ever really said much to him about his classroom. As a new teacher, he had come in with high ideals and spent countless hours going through the book and developing notes and activities for the students. But, over the years, the activities had disappeared until all that was left was what was easy—pulling out the notes each time. Mrs. Sanders asked him about the pacing guide for the course, and he shook his head. Coach Morgan could not remember the last time he had looked at the pacing guide from the state—again, no one had ever seemed interested in how he performed in the classroom, so he spent his time and energy on the football field.

Mrs. Sanders nodded. She explained to Coach Morgan that she knew and respected that he was a legendary football coach. At the same time, she explained that the students in his classes deserved to have that same level of focus and determination that he showed on the football field. Coach Morgan agreed. Mrs. Sanders said that she planned to talk with all of the US history teachers about the pacing guide and working together to ensure that all of them were following it. While Coach Morgan's test scores were lower than the others, there was room for improvement for all of Torrance's US history teachers.

Mrs. Sanders told the coach that she felt that working together to tackle the pacing of the course and developing some newer, standards-based lessons would benefit all of the teachers and the students. The group could divide the work so that no one teacher was having to create everything. Coach Morgan agreed that he would work with the group of teachers to improve the instruction in the US history course. Mrs. Sanders nodded—she told him she needed him, as someone that the other teachers respected and would follow—and the students needed him as well. Coach Morgan has to learn innovative ways to teach the US history curriculum in order to improve assessment scores.

Questions for Discussion

1. What positive things did Mrs. Sanders see in Coach Morgan's classroom? What negatives did she see?
2. How did (or does) Coach Morgan set a purpose and direction for the lesson in the classroom?
3. How does Coach Morgan interact with students in the classroom? What are his strengths and weaknesses in terms of student interactions?
4. What does Mrs. Sanders do to address the issues that she saw with Coach Morgan's instruction? What do you think of her approach?
5. In general, what can new administrators do to address issues with veteran teachers without making the veteran teachers feel disrespected?
6. Are there other suggestions you would make for Mrs. Sanders or to Coach Morgan?

CASE STUDY 1.3
OBSERVATIONS AND STUDENT OUTCOMES

Standards 3.a and 4.f

Topic: Urban high school. This is a case about Formative Assessment. The assistant principal prepares a teacher who has evaluations tied to students' test scores.

Mrs. Dukes has been the evaluator and supervisor for Mr. Randal for three years. She enjoys observing his classroom. Mrs. Dukes hired Mr. Randal for a math teaching position when she interviewed him three years ago. His enthusiasm and desire to make a difference for students, as well as his dual certifications in math and special education, impressed Mrs. Dukes. Teachers like Mr. Randal are needed desperately in her school.

Crossroads High School serves a portion of a large metropolitan area. Luckily, crime rates are not high in the community around Crossroads, which is an older, established community in the city. However, the population can be somewhat transient as there are many rental properties, and the students are mainly from lower socioeconomic backgrounds. The Crossroads community is also majority minority. The school serves 2,500 students, 40 percent of whom are African American and 25 percent of whom are Hispanic. Mr. Randal is an African American male teacher with a degree in math education and a Master's degree in special education. Mrs. Dukes felt that he was the perfect fit for Crossroads when she hired him.

Now, three years later, Mrs. Dukes continues to feel that Mr. Randal is a good fit. He serves as an assistant football and track coach, and volunteers in the mentoring program. Mrs. Dukes often sees Mr. Randal talking with students—especially young men—in the hallway about their grades, their behaviors, and how things are going in their lives in general. The students have responded well to Mr. Randal, and he is definitely someone that the students admire and respect.

Over the past three years, however, Mr. Randal's test scores have not been very good. His students do not perform as well on the end-of-year state tests as the students of other teachers in the building. Mrs. Dukes, an assistant principal, has been instructed by her principal to speak with Mr. Randal about the test scores and come up with an action plan. This will be in the best interest of both the students and Mr. Randal because Mr. Randal's evaluation score is tied to his students' test scores. If they don't do well, he will receive lower marks on his evaluation.

Mrs. Dukes is not sure, though, how to approach this issue. She has observed Mr. Randal in the classroom for the past three years, and he has received high marks on his observations. He does focus on teaching the math standards and includes the standard and an essential question on the board each day to focus the students' attention. He also does a great job of supporting students in the classroom.

Mr. Randal works with students when they don't understand the content, leading them through multiple examples and modeling how to solve the math problems. He is encouraging, and the rapport that he has built with students outside of class is evident in the classroom as well. So, Mrs. Dukes is not sure why there is a disconnect between what she has observed and the final test scores. When she is observing, Mr. Randal's students show understanding of the content standards and seem able to solve the problems presented to them. The test scores do not reflect that.

During the pre-evaluation conference at the beginning of the year, Mrs. Dukes discusses the test scores with Mr. Randal, and she shares her confusion over why the students didn't perform better. Mr. Randal also shares her confusion, and his disappointment that his students are not performing as well as their peers in the school. He assures Mrs. Dukes that he will do whatever he needs to do and he is open to feedback and suggestions. He asks her which teachers in the math department had higher test scores so that he can go and talk with them about what they do and also observe them during his planning period.

Mrs. Dukes agrees that this is a good plan, and she tells him to visit the department chair, Mr. Lory, whose students excelled on the assessments. Mrs. Dukes also tells him that she plans to observe him a couple of times during the first few weeks of the school year to try to see if there are any suggestions she can make about his lessons.

Mrs. Dukes does observe Mr. Randal two times during the first six weeks of school. She makes extensive notes during her observations about how Mr. Randal presents the lesson content and skills to the students, the number of practice problems that the class does, and the number of problems that the students are asked to do independently. She also makes notes of the interactions between Mr. Randal and the students—noting when they ask him for help, how he responds, and whether they are able to solve the problem after his intervention.

In addition to observing Mr. Randal, Mrs. Dukes also spends time observing Mr. Lory, the math department chair who has excellent assessment scores. She makes the same type of extensive notes in his classroom. After observing both teachers and gathering her notes, Mrs. Dukes spends time rereading her notes and looking for any patterns. One afternoon in the quiet of her office, after everyone else has left for the day, Mrs. Dukes believes that she has finally put the puzzle pieces together.

The next morning, Mrs. Dukes schedules a conference with Mr. Randal for later that afternoon. When he comes to her office, he again expresses his desire to improve and says that he has enjoyed observing Mr. Lory and talking to him about teaching. He shares with Mrs. Dukes that one thing he has noticed is that Mr. Lory pushes the students to do things independently.

"He doesn't help them when it's time for them to work problems by themselves," explains Mr. Randal. "At first, I thought it was mean! They would ask him to help them, and he would say no—they needed to work it out themselves first and then he would discuss it with them."

Mrs. Dukes smiles slightly and nods, "So you thought it was mean—I can see that. What do you think now?"

"Well, after talking with Mr. Lory about it, I can see why he does it. He says that the students will use the teacher as a crutch if they can. When something is difficult, they don't want to persevere. They want us to help them and 'hold their hands' so that they don't have to do hard things. Mr. Lory doesn't let them use him as a crutch. He makes them struggle with the content on their own a little so that he builds their ability to be independent. It still bothers me a little not to help the students when they first ask, but I am trying to take a step back and let them know that I want to see what they can do without me. I have told my students in the past couple of days that there will be times when I am not there to help them, and they have to figure out how they are going to do it then."

Mrs. Dukes smiles. "What's funny is that's the exact same thing that I discovered when I reviewed my notes after observing the two of you! I noticed that the students were actually never required to solve things independently. Even when they had independent problems, they could always call on you to help them work through the problem. So, while it looked like they were developing understanding, it only went so far. I think this is why there is a disconnect between what I have observed and the test scores. They can't ask for you to give them tips and reminders during the test. They have to work independently!"

Mr. Randal nods. "I agree. I am still working on taking that step back, but I do see that it is necessary if my students are going to develop independent math skills."

Questions for Discussion

1. Why did Mrs. Dukes think that Mr. Randal was a "good fit" for Crossroads High School?
2. The test scores of Mr. Randal's students affect his evaluation score. What do you think about this? Is it fair for a teacher to be directly tied to how his or her students perform on a standardized test at the end of the year? What percentage of the evaluation should be tied to test scores—what's fair?
3. Mrs. Dukes asks Mr. Randal to observe another math teacher who has higher test scores. What do you think about this approach? What might be some pros and potential cons of this plan?
4. Mrs. Dukes spends time observing Mr. Randal, gathering extensive notes, and then observing another math teacher with higher test scores. What do you think about this approach? What other strategies for addressing this problem might Mrs. Dukes have used?
5. Mrs. Dukes and Mr. Randal arrive at the same conclusion—that students are not working independently enough. What do you think of this? Do you think they are on to something or do you think they need to continue to look for root causes?
6. Discuss Mr. Randal's attitude toward his low test scores and improving his practice. How does his attitude make a difference in this situation? As an administrator, how might you handle this situation differently if the teacher were resistant to the conversation?

Chapter Two

Classroom Management

CASE STUDY 2.1
CONSISTENCY IS KEY

Standards 4.a and 4.c

Topic: Elementary school. This is a case about the school principal setting expectations and procedures for a rural elementary school teacher.

Mr. Pope glanced out the window of his office as the old cottonwood tree rustled harshly in the wind. He had been an assistant principal at Cottonwood Elementary for two years. It was November and time to complete his first round of observations. He sighed and ran his hand through his thinning black hair as he stood up to walk down the wide hallway of the first-grade wing. Today he was supposed to observe Miss Figg, and he was anxious about it.

Miss Figg was a new teacher, hired in September. She was fresh-faced and newly out of college. In fact, Mr. Pope had been excited about hiring her. Miss Figg had grown up in the small town of Cottonwood and knew the rural population she was dealing with. At the time, he had appreciated her understanding of the area, as well as her enthusiasm for the position. However, by October, things with Miss Figg seemed to be falling apart. She was constantly sending kids to his office for discipline issues. Often, the issues were relatively minor: an out-of-uniform child or a student chewing gum. Sometimes, the issues were bigger: a fight in her room or cursing at the teacher.

Mr. Pope had just had a discussion with the principal that morning about Miss Figg. Clearly, things were going amiss in her classroom. The question was why. It wasn't surprising, really. Many new teachers struggled, especially with the population at Cottonwood.

A small farm community, Cottonwood was very rural. Many of the residents worked blue-collar jobs or were out of work completely, but that wasn't the problem. The problem was drugs. Like many places in the country, Cottonwood had recently had an outbreak in crystal meth production and consumption. Some of the students' parents were in jail for drugs, and many more lived in homes where meth was being used. Needless to say, many of these kids did not have stable home lives, which had a direct impact on their behavior in school.

As he pushed open the heavy beige door to the first-grade classroom, he was greeted with Miss Figg's brightly decorated classroom. Purple and blue paper bordered every bulletin board, and large classroom posters said inspirational messages like, "Today is a great day to learn something new."

On her white board, at the front of the classroom, Miss Figg had done everything the school had asked of her. She had written the date and the learning objective for every lesson, including the lesson Mr. Pope was observing: reading. In her lesson plan, which she had submitted to Mr. Pope the night before, she had carefully aligned this objective with a first-grade Common Core standard. In addition, she had also aligned the lesson with a social studies standard.

As Mr. Pope settled himself down at the back of Miss Figg's classroom, he stopped to watch what was happening. Miss Figg had twenty-five first graders in her classroom. She stood at the front of the room, her blonde head bobbing, as she attempted to transition the kids from math to reading. "Okay class," she said. "We are going to put our math papers in our math folders. I want you to get out your reading folders now." Mr. Pope heard her say this over the buzzing of laughter and talking in the classroom, but just barely. After saying this, only a small handful of students put away their green math folders.

"Miss Figg," yelled a little freckled boy at the front of the classroom. "Which one is my math folder again?"

"The green one," Miss Figg replied. The little boy continued to rummage through a very messy desk while the rest of the class continued its commotion. In fact, the sound got louder as Miss Figg's face got redder; she stood planted like a statue at the front of the classroom.

After some more confused shouts about the folders and a series of kids getting up to sharpen their pencils, one little girl shouted that she needed to use the restroom. Miss Figg quickly gave her the pass and shouted above the roar of the class, "I need your attention! Today we are going to learn about retelling a story." She pointed at the objective as she said this, but few kids looked up. Mr. Pope glanced at his watch; seven minutes had gone by since he'd entered the classroom.

After reviewing the objective, Miss Figg asked the class what it meant to make a story map. A pigtailed girl answered, and Miss Figg seemed satisfied and moved on. The rest of the class appeared not to hear. She then brought out a beautiful book, *Mufaro's Beautiful Daughters*.

"Class," Miss Figg said. "I'd like you all to move to the reading rug." Twenty of the twenty-five kids then sprang up and ran to a cozy purple rug dotted with several pillows and beanbags while five kids lingered at their desks.

Miss Figg repeated her request to the desk sitters, and two kids broke out in a loud argument over a pillow on the rug. Miss Figg, quite flustered at this point, shouted at the kids to stop and ran over to break it up. She sent one to time-out; the other remained seated on the rug and eventually the argued-over pillow. Meanwhile, another girl shouted she wanted to use the restroom, and two kids tried to sharpen pencils. The previous girl who'd used the bathroom came back in and started throwing crayons at a friend.

"Now is not the time to use the restroom," she retorted to the little girl who wanted to go to the bathroom. "Stop sharpening pencils!" she yelled at the kids at the pencil sharpener. After that, the classroom quieted down a little bit. She brought the student back from time-out, and Miss Figg settled down to read.

Mr. Pope glanced at his watch again. Another six minutes had gone by. At this point, Miss Figg held up the book and asked the students to turn to their neighbors and tell them one thing they noticed about the book. Next, she asked them to make a prediction about the story. Most of the students participated in this portion of the class, and Miss Figg listened to the buzz of conversation from her rocking chair at the edge of the rug. To gauge the class's reaction, she pulled popsicle sticks, each with a student's name on it, from a can and asked about the answers with which they came up.

After asking a few more questions and identifying Zimbabwe (where the story takes place) on a map, Miss Figg began to read the story. In the beginning, almost all of the students were completely enamored by the book. By the end, however, several had begun to chatter in the back of the rug. Miss Figg just read louder. She stopped at several sections of the book to have her students turn and talk to their neighbors about a question she would pose. Each time, this seemed to refocus her class.

After reading, Miss Figg asked the students how they knew the book took place in Africa. Again, she used the turn-and-talk method. This time, one of the little boys who had been in the arguing match waved his arm frantically in the air to be called on. As he answered, the little girl who'd asked to go to the bathroom before started wiggling. "Go!" Miss Figg said in a hushed whisper. The little girl ran out of the room without a hall pass.

Another twenty minutes had gone by, and Miss Figg's forty-five-minute lesson was almost over. He could tell that she was trying to rush to the end. "Go back to your seats," she instructed the students. Again, there was a large commotion as students pushed desks and shouted across the room. Several kids got up to sharpen pencils again. After five minutes, Miss Figg had the class settled back in their seats, but there was still a low conversation going on toward the back. Miss Figg ignored it and began passing out a blank sheet of paper.

She spent the next ten minutes trying to explain how to fold the paper so that there were six boxes in which to do their story map. She rushed around the room trying to help kids individually as they struggled. Finally, one of the students shouted, "Miss Figg! It's lunch time!" She glanced at the clock on the wall and seemed to have just noticed it was two minutes past!

"Students!" she said. "Put your story maps in your reading folder and line up!" Most kids stuffed the sheets in a messy desk and sprinted to a small cluster at the door. She let them all out, and they walked in a noisy clump toward the lunch room.

The next day, during Miss Figg's planning period, she came to see Mr. Pope in his office to discuss the observation. Prior to the meeting, Mr. Pope had decided there were several things he noticed about Miss Figg's lesson that he'd change in order to better suit the needs of the students. However, he decided to focus on one or two things in order to not overwhelm her, especially since this was her first observation. The last thing he wanted was for her to quit because the job was too difficult. Like most administrators, Mr. Pope had once been a first-year teacher himself. He remembered all too well that the learning curve was steep.

After complimenting Miss Figg on the content of the lesson, he then focused on the main thing he wanted Miss Figg to change: class routines and expectations. "In your ideal world, what would happen each time a kid wanted to answer a question or line up for lunch?" he asked. Miss Figg went on to describe how students would raise their hands to ask questions and line up quietly in a line when they went to lunch.

After discussing several routines, including how she addressed class discipline, Mr. Pope suggested that she write these out. "You should have a procedure for everything," Mr. Pope said.

"The kids should know exactly what is expected from them when they do everything from sharpen a pencil to go to the bathroom." He went on to describe how their students' lives were unstable at home, so stability and clear expectations in the classroom were even more important. He suggested going through these procedures prior to each transition and activity.

"Before you go to the reading corner, review with them how you want them to get there and how they should act once they're seated. You'd be surprised by how much they just don't realize on their own." He also pointed out that her discipline procedure needed to be more consistent. "When the two kids got in the skirmish, you did not discipline the same," he pointed out.

Miss Figg went back to her classroom and wrote each procedure out. She then kept this list in her lesson plan binder to remind her. For the next week, she went over these procedures several times each day with the students and would remind them again if someone did not do as expected. She posted several commonly used transitions and procedures on large posters in her room. To her surprise, things in her classroom did start to get easier. It wasn't perfect, but the kids' awareness of expectations increased and the visits to Mr. Pope's office were far less frequent.

Questions for Discussion

1. What did you see Miss Figg do well?
2. Why do you think the better system of expectations helped Miss Figg?
3. How can Mr. Pope support the young teacher past the observation? What can he do to ensure that he is checking in with her?
4. What other problems did you notice in Miss Figg's lesson? Do you agree with Mr. Pope's decision not to point out every problem? Why or why not?
5. What can administrators do, in general, to help new teachers like Miss Figg?
6. Are there any other suggestions you'd make to Miss Figg? What's the next thing you would address?

CASE STUDY 2.2
INDEPENDENT GROUP WORK

Standards 2.c and 4.c

Topic: Elementary school. This is a case about group work strategies. A teacher learns to set clear expectations for group work.

Mrs. Waters walked out of her office at Newbridge Elementary and let her clerk know that she would be observing classrooms. Newbridge Elementary served a population of 550 students in a suburban community. Situated not far from a mid-sized town, Newbridge was a "bedroom" community for many young professionals who worked in the nearby town. The students at Newbridge were relatively diverse for the area, with 63 percent being white, 24 percent African American, 10 percent Hispanic, and 3 percent other races. Approximately 30 percent of the students qualified for free or reduced lunch.

The faculty at Newbridge was relatively stable, and many teachers began their careers in the community and retired there. This year, Newbridge hired only three new teachers due to two retirements and one relocation. Mrs. Waters was pleased with how her new teachers were fitting in at Newbridge, and she attributed their easy assimilation to the grade-level professional learning communities. At Newbridge, each grade level was expected to work as a team—planning lessons together, giving some common assessments, and working to meet the needs of all of the students as a team. Today, Mrs. Waters was planning to visit the fourth-grade classroom of Ms. Ruff, one of her new teachers.

As Mrs. Waters entered the classroom, she noticed that students were in groups; according to the daily schedule on the board, these were literature circles. Mrs. Waters also noticed the tidiness of the classroom and the arrangement of workspaces for the students. Ms. Ruff's "area"—her desk, computer, filing cabinets, and so on—was contained in one corner of the room, and all of the other space was dedicated to students. Student desks were arranged to make tables for the groups, a "reading tent" was arranged in one corner with pillows and a shelf filled with books, and another space held cubbies and hooks for student belongings. Mrs. Waters made note of the vibrant posters on the walls that outlined the rules for the classroom and the use of the bulletin board to highlight student work.

Mrs. Waters focused her attention on observing the literature circles in the room. She could see that the groups were reading books on the upcoming state assessment. The group closest to her was reading *Where the Red Fern Grows*, and they had a worksheet with questions to complete as they read. Another group to her other side was reading *Sarah, Plain and Tall*, and they also had a worksheet with questions to answer. Ms. Ruff circulated from group to group, stopping to listen to their conversations and join in as she had an interesting question or comment. As she continued to watch the groups, Mrs. Waters noticed that the noise level in the room was surprisingly low. In her experience, groups typically made more noise than this, and the room was relatively quiet for students to be working together in groups.

As she watched, Mrs. Waters realized why it was so quiet. The groups interacted infrequently. She noticed that the groups closest to her were reading independently and answering the questions independently. The only interaction that she observed in one group was when one of the students was not sure what to write down, and she asked another student. In the other group, she noticed two of the boys snickering and playing with a small toy, but no other interactions occurred related to the book. Mrs. Waters did observe one group from across the room. That group appeared to be reading a few pages independently and then stopping to talk about what they had read and answer questions. The only group that was continually making any noise or interacting was a group that had decided to read the chapter aloud by taking turns. They were reading aloud, although quietly enough to try not to interrupt the other groups.

The groups did interact when Ms. Ruff approached them, stopping their reading to answer her questions or respond to her comments. Mrs. Waters observed that Ms. Ruff asked the groups closest to her to tell her what they were reading and then she asked them what they had gotten for the answers on the worksheet so far. As Mrs. Waters listened, she realized that the two groups had a similar set of generic questions about their books—the questions were not specific to the book. She wrote down two of the questions that she had heard in the discussion from both groups: Summarize what happened in this chapter. What did you learn about the main character in this chapter?

Toward the end of the observation, Ms. Ruff brought Mrs. Waters a lesson plan with the worksheet attached. "I thought you might want to see what they are doing," Ms. Ruff explained. Mrs. Waters reviewed the lesson plan, which stated that the students were in literature circles based on Lexile level and interest in the various books that were offered as a choice. The worksheet, as Mrs. Waters had already surmised, was the same for each group. It was a set of generic questions that the students could answer about any fiction text they might be reading.

Ms. Ruff came to see Mrs. Waters the following day during her planning time. Mrs. Waters smiled at Ms. Ruff when she walked in. "How is your year going so far?"

"Great!" Ms. Ruff offered. "I really enjoy my students, and my team has been so helpful. The literature circles were actually Mr. Cross's idea. He uses them in his classroom, and I thought I would give it a try."

Mrs. Waters nodded and asked Ms. Ruff to share the goal of the literature circles—what students should get out of the activity.

"Well, it allows for me to differentiate based on their reading levels and their interests. Instead of all reading the same book, there are some choices. Also, it gives them a chance to interact and discuss what they are reading instead of just reading by themselves."

Mrs. Waters agreed with these stated goals of the literature circles. "What standards are you hoping to address with the literature circles? What reading standards should students be covering?"

Ms. Ruff hesitated. "Well, they are learning about character and why characters make the choices they make. They are also learning about authors' choices, and they are practicing reading comprehension skills—summarizing, finding the main idea or theme, and making predictions. The worksheets that they had have some questions on there about all of these things."

Mrs. Waters agreed that she had viewed the worksheet and had seen those types of questions. "Describe the perfect literature circle to me," Mrs. Waters asked. "What are the students doing and learning?"

Ms. Ruff explained, "The students are engaging in a discussion of what they read. They share their opinions about what has happened, what will happen next, and what a character should do. To me, it's almost like a book club. They are able to express how they are feeling about reading the book and where the plot of the story is going. They aren't just summarizing on the paper or making predictions so that I can read them later. They are discussing their thoughts with each other and helping each other grow as readers."

Mrs. Waters smiled, "Which of your groups was doing that during today's lesson?"

Ms. Ruff hesitated. "Honestly, I am not sure any of them were," she began, but rushed on to say, "But we just started doing the literature circles, so I think they are still getting used to them."

"What type of instruction have you given the students on literature circles and what they should be doing in their groups?"

Ms. Ruff admitted that she had not given the students much. Students had been told they would work together in a literature circle. Then, the groups chose a book and received the worksheet. Ms. Ruff admitted that she had not really talked to them much further about her expectations for how they would interact and work together.

Mrs. Waters agreed with her. "The students were sitting together, but they rarely interacted or discussed like you describe in your description of the perfect literature circle. I think they aren't sure how to do that or what you expect. They are reading and working independently even while sitting with their groups." Ms. Ruff nodded. "So, what could you do to make sure they understand how to function as a literature circle?"

Ms. Ruff thought for a minute. "I have a book about literature circles that talks about giving each student a role in the group—the leader, the time keeper, the drawer, the page finder. I could start with giving them some roles to fulfill in their groups."

Mrs. Waters agreed that would be a good start. "I would also talk with them about your expectation that they discuss what they have read. While your generic list of questions is okay, many of them only require lower-order thinking skills like recalling what they read. There aren't really any questions that could generate the type of discussion you describe."

"So," Ms. Ruff surmised, "I should include some questions on the worksheets that could generate a debate or discussion?"

Mrs. Waters nodded. "I think that would be a good start and would help you realize your goal of having students interact and learn together as they read. So, you have two things to implement pretty quickly to improve the literature circles—give the students roles to fulfill as part of a group and include some higher-order questions for the groups so that interaction and discussion will be encouraged."

A week later, Mrs. Waters was walking down the fourth-grade hallway, and she could hear Ms. Ruff's students as she passed the door. She paused to stick her head into the classroom. What she witnessed made her smile. The students were again working in their literature circles, but the interaction level was very different. The groups were coming to the end of their books, and they had been asked to cast the movie version of the book. They had to choose which actors would play the various characters in the book. The students were engaged in lively conversations around which actors would be best, and they were citing characteristics of the characters to support their responses or refute someone else's. While she watched, a boy in one group said to his team, "Time—that's all the time we have to spend on that character. We need to move on to the next one."

Ms. Ruff came over when she saw Mrs. Waters. "This is great!" she said. "Ever since I gave them roles and also thought about what type of questions would generate more discussion, these literature circles have been so much better. The kids are really getting into their books, and it's like they can't wait to come in and talk with each other about what they are reading. That was the goal all along!"

Questions for Discussion

1. What structures are in place at the school to support new teachers? As an administrator, what else would you put into place to support new teachers like Ms. Ruff?
2. What positive things could Mrs. Waters point out to Ms. Ruff after the observation? What negative things?
3. Why weren't Ms. Ruff's literature circle groups interacting the way that she envisioned?
4. What do you think of how Mrs. Waters approached the issue with Ms. Ruff? As an administrator, what might you do differently?
5. Putting students into groups to work seems like an easy task, but most teachers and administrators say that it takes more planning than teaching the whole class. Why do you think planning for groups is so important? Can you think of a time when putting students into a group (besides testing) would not be the best approach?
6. What other suggestions or supports might you have for Ms. Ruff if you were her administrator?

CASE STUDY 2.3
WIGGLE WORMS

Standards 4.c and 4.d

Topic: Elementary school. Mr. Quinn, a first-year elementary school teacher, struggles with age-appropriate instruction during a math lesson.

Mrs. Piper had been an administrator at Lovejoy Elementary for ten years, and she absolutely loved her job. She could think of no other profession where she could spend the day surrounded by the excitement and wonder of children, while at the same time feeling like she was making a profound difference in their lives. Mrs. Piper prided herself on the positive climate at Lovejoy. She worked to hire teachers who shared her belief that teaching young children was a calling, and she worked to build positive relationships with her faculty, the students, and their parents.

Lovejoy served a rural community. Forestry was the biggest industry for the county. Most of the parents of her four hundred students either worked in the forestry industry or commuted to work in the next county, where there was a mid-sized town. While her students were mostly white, 86 percent of them to be exact, most of her students were also economically disadvantaged. A total of 78 percent of the students at Lovejoy qualified for free or reduced price lunch. Mrs. Piper knew that many of her students went home to mobile homes at night, many to single-parent households or to their grandparents.

Some of her young students experienced very little stability in their lives, as alcoholism and drug abuse were two major issues facing the rural community. Mrs. Piper had worked to make sure that her faculty understood the environment surrounding their school. She had even gone so far as to have the faculty take a bus tour of the county during preplanning so that the teachers could see the homes of the students firsthand. Mrs. Piper stressed to her faculty the need to create a positive, loving environment for students, where consistency reigned.

Mr. Quinn was a first-year teacher at Lovejoy, having recently graduated from the small community college two counties over. He had grown up in a small, rural community, and he wanted to "return to his roots," or so he explained to Mrs. Piper during his interview. He was also offered a position helping to coach the county's high school baseball team, which cemented his decision to work at Lovejoy. Mrs. Piper was planning to spend some time observing Mr. Quinn this morning as part of the annual evaluation process.

Mrs. Piper loved visiting kindergarten classrooms. While teachers might be able to "put on a show" in some of the older grades, it was much more difficult for them to try to deviate from their normal practice in kindergarten. The younger students responded to routines and expectations so well that it was easy to recognize when they had not been set. As Mrs. Piper entered Mr. Quinn's room, she could see evidence that he had worked to establish procedures and routines in the classroom. She noticed a behavior "stoplight" that was similar to what some of the other teachers in kindergarten used.

Students started the day on "green," but if they needed a consequence for a behavior choice, their individual clips could be moved off of green to yellow and then to red as needed. Mrs. Piper also noticed the daily schedule chart at the front of the room, which was another staple in her kindergarten classrooms. The chart outlined the daily schedule for the class, and it had a giant colored clip on the side that the teacher or a student could move down as they completed each activity. Mr. Quinn's class was on "Core Math" when Mrs. Piper entered the room.

Mr. Quinn was working with the students on recognizing "one more or one less." The standard was a very early introduction of addition and subtraction. Mr. Quinn was using manipulatives with the students, and each student had a baggie full of small colored disks. Mr. Quinn asked each student to count out a certain number of disks, such as five disks or eight disks. Then he asked them to count out "one more" and write down the answer or "one less" and write down the answer. The students appeared to be enjoying the lesson and engaging with it, as they diligently counted out their disks and added "one more" or took away a disk so they would have "one less."

Mrs. Piper enjoyed the looks on the students' faces as they engaged with the lesson. However, as the lesson went on—the "instruction" with manipulatives lasted for twenty-five minutes according to Mrs. Piper's watch—Mrs. Piper noticed a decreasing level of engagement. As Mr. Quinn presented problem after problem for the students to count out, some students seemed to lose interest. One young boy began to line up all of the disks in his baggie so he could see how many disks he had in all. A young lady was stacking her disks in a "tower." Two students were swapping disks because one wanted more blue disks and one wanted more red ones.

After twenty-five minutes, Mr. Quinn praised the students on their new addition and subtraction skills, and the class had a "mini-celebration of learning." The students all gave themselves a round of applause. Then Mr. Quinn took up the manipulatives and passed out a worksheet with additional "one more" or "one less" problems on it. The front side had ten "one more" problems, and the back side had ten "one less" problems on it. Mr. Quinn asked the students to practice their math skills by completing the worksheet. He began to circulate around the tables of students to offer assistance or to praise them for their work.

A few of the students immediately started to work, but Mrs. Piper noticed that many students did not. At the table closest to her, a young lady stood up and walked over to Mrs. Piper. "What are you doing?" the girl asked.

"I am just watching to see what you are learning," Mrs. Piper replied.

"Oh," said the girl. "Your dress is very pretty. I like blue."

Mr. Quinn noticed and said, "Anna, you need to practice your math, please." The girl moved back to her seat, but she did not begin working. Instead, she smiled at Mrs. Piper and kept looking at her.

Mrs. Piper noticed that other students also seemed to want to get up and move around the room. Two students asked Mr. Quinn if they could go to the bathroom. Another student told Mr. Quinn that his pencil was in his backpack. Another student told Mr. Quinn that she had a hurt finger and she wanted to go see the nurse. Mr. Quinn had to redirect several students for talking or giggling at their tables instead of working through the math problems. Each time, these students were directed to move their clips on the traffic light. Mrs. Piper observed the independent math practice for approximately twenty minutes before she finalized the observation and left the room. During the twenty minutes of independent practice, nine students had been asked to move their clips down to yellow or to red.

Mr. Quinn visited Mrs. Piper after school that day to review the observation. Mrs. Piper began with the positive things she had noticed while in Mr. Quinn's classroom. She knew that as a brand new teacher, Mr. Quinn needed positive encouragement as well as constructive criticism. After praising Mr. Quinn for the positives she had noticed, Mrs. Piper brought his attention to the issues that she noticed that needed to be addressed.

Questions for Discussion

1. What does Mr. Quinn do well in his classroom?
2. What about Mr. Quinn's lesson plan triggered misbehavior in his students?
3. Come up with a list of action steps for working with Mr. Quinn. Give reasons for your steps.
4. Teachers are under increasing pressure to focus on academic skills, even with young students. As an administrator, how would you help teachers to balance rigorous academic standards with developmentally appropriate activities for children?
5. How can Mr. Quinn set high expectations for his students in accordance with their needs and abilities? Do you have any other suggestions for Mr. Quinn for the upcoming years if he is to continuously improve as a teacher?

CASE STUDY 2.4
SPIRALING DOWN THE GOSSIP STAIRCASE

Standards 3.d and 3.g

Topic: Urban elementary school. This is a case about classroom management and discipline. Mr. O'Toole, a paraprofessional, allows for a proliferation of behavioral issues to occur in his fifth-grade classroom.

River Academy is an urban non-profit kindergarten to sixth-grade elementary charter school located in New Haven, Connecticut. River Academy serves approximately 210 students. There is one class per grade level with a lead certified teacher and a full-time paraprofessional in each classroom. Part of the role of the paraprofessional is to assist the teacher in the classroom and supervise the students during lunch, recess, and specials. In this school year, the Board of Directors promoted Lakisha Rasheed, the former fourth-grade teacher, to the newly created position of assistant principal. Mrs. Rasheed handles the day-to-day school operations while the principal, Brian Shaughnessy, focuses on opening up a second elementary school.

Even though Mrs. Rasheed was a first-year administrator, she had managed to earn the respect of most staff members by establishing an open culture where ideas and opinions were welcome and collaboration encouraged. Many parents also respected Mrs. Rasheed because their students had previously been in her class and she was known to have a no-nonsense, strict, but fair discipline style.

Five years previous to Mrs. Rasheed becoming assistant principal, Brian Shaughnessy had become principal of River Academy. When Mr. Shaughnessy took over, there was lying and stealing between staff members, teachers teaching with expired licenses, and favoritism, just to name a few problems. Mr. Shaughnessy made the difficult choice to fire longtime staff members in order to improve the morale of the school. After five years of letting go numerous staff members and making changes to the business structure of the school, there was finally a strong culture of trust, and the staff members were eager to come to work every day.

In August of this year, the fifth-grade paraprofessional who had recently been hired left for a higher-paying job a week before school started. Mrs. Rasheed saw this as her first major problem to solve as an administrator. "Don't panic," she repeated to herself over and over as she attempted to find qualified candidates ready to work on such short notice. On "meet the teacher" night, she reassured the concerned fifth-grade parents not to worry, there would be a full-time paraprofessional present on the first day of school. Two days before the start of school, Mrs. Rasheed hired Caleb O'Toole, a friend of Mr. Shaughnessy's daughter, to be the paraprofessional. He seemed to be the perfect fit for the job.

Caleb O'Toole was a certified secondary education teacher who had recently graduated college but had no luck finding a teaching job. He completed his internship in a New Haven public school that had a reputation for rough student behaviors. Mrs. Rasheed was confident that if he could handle those high school students, fifth grade would be a walk in the park for him. However, as the school year went on, more and more issues seemed to arise when the students were under his supervision.

The school year started off on a great note. The lead teacher established clear expectations and consequences. She was known to have excellent classroom management and rarely had to send students to the office. The students were excited to have Mr. O'Toole as a paraprofessional, as the only other male in the building was the physical education teacher. Many of the students were growing up in single-mother households and looked up to him as a positive male role model. However, by November, the lead teacher began expressing concerns to Mrs. Rasheed that when the students were supervised by him, there was often chaos. Mrs. Rasheed decided to conduct informal observations when Mr. O'Toole was supervising the students.

Between November and April, Mrs. Rasheed dealt with a range of behavior issues with the fifth-grade class such as fighting, inappropriate language, lying, and insubordination. As she looked back over her notes, she noticed they all had one thing in common: Mr. O'Toole was the primary supervisor during all the incidents. When Mrs. Rasheed talked to Mr. O'Toole about the issues, he seemed to be aware and agreed to work on his classroom management skills. During this time, other staff members were also beginning to pick up on his relaxed approach.

Then one day in May, Mrs. Rasheed had just sat down in her office from greeting all the students as they entered the building when a fifth-grade father, Mr. Jones, came storming into her office, clearly upset, with his daughter, Savannah, trailing behind him. She quickly did her best to calm him down while she asked the student to wait in the hallway. In a rage, Mr. Jones stated that when Savannah came home from school the previous day, she confided in him that Mr. O'Toole had hit her on the back at around 10 a.m. when he became upset with her for leaving the classroom to go to her locker in the hallway.

Mr. O'Toole had been substitute teaching while the lead teacher was absent. Mr. Jones stated that he wanted the Board of Directors phone numbers to ensure that Mr. O'Toole was fired over the incident. However, Mrs. Rasheed stated that she is not allowed to give out such contact information in order to respect their privacy. She assured him that she would investigate and get to the bottom of the issue and contact him when a decision was made.

Mrs. Rasheed spent the rest of the morning talking with Savannah and then Mr. O'Toole to get their sides of the story. Mr. O'Toole stated that she did in fact get up and leave without permission around 10 a.m. When he went out to the hallway to get her, she was standing at her locker and ignored his directions to get back into the room. After a brief argument, she started to walk to the room and he gently placed his hand on her upper back to guide her there. When Mrs. Rasheed talked with Savannah, she stuck with the story that her dad had told.

But as Mrs. Rasheed talked with her more and more, Savannah confessed that she made up the story to avoid getting into trouble over leaving the classroom without permission. Mrs. Rasheed was relieved that the incident was over and called Mr. Jones to share the news. But instead of Mr. Jones expressing relief that the story was false, he instead became more upset and accused Mrs. Rasheed of making Savannah falsely confess in order to protect

Mr. O'Toole. When Mrs. Rasheed left school that evening, her mind was racing trying to figure out her next move.

As Mrs. Rasheed entered her office the next morning, she was shocked to find her answering machine full of messages. It seemed that Mr. Jones had told other parents that Mr. O'Toole hit his child and the school was not taking action. Worse, rumors were starting to circulate among staff members that Mr. O'Toole had hit a student and he wasn't fired because he was a male in a school dominated by females. It seemed that the positive culture Mrs. Rasheed had worked all year to build was crashing down. However, she didn't have time to address any rumors because she had scheduled another meeting with Mr. Jones, Mr. O'Toole, and Savannah.

Mr. Jones had a grueling two-hour meeting separately with all those involved. He learned that Savannah had lied in order to avoid trouble before. It appeared she had a history of doing so at school and home. He agreed that the issue needed to be settled sooner rather than later.

Questions for Discussion:

1. What is the next step that Mr. Jones needs to take? Why?
2. Should school administrators be required to provide the Board of Directors' contact information to parents?
3. Should there be a system of accountability for paraprofessionals like there are with certified teachers in the building?
4. What kind of support should be offered to students in these types of situations?
5. Should the situation have been discussed with other staff members and/or parents in order to stop the spreading of rumors?
6. What steps did Mrs. Rasheed take in order to deescalate the situations and make sure everyone's story was heard?
7. What could have been done differently to resolve this issue? Why?

Chapter Three

Distinctive Student Abilities

CASE STUDY 3.1
ACCOMMODATIONS ARE KEY

Standards 2.c, 4.c, 5.c

Topic: Suburban high school. Hana is a student attending Independent High School with one special education teacher in the building with an Individualized Education Plan (IEP) in a tenth-grade science lesson on chemical reactions. This is about school leaders ensuring that all teachers understand the requirements of IEPs.

Mr. Gregory was surprised to see Hana in his office. She had never been in trouble during the year and a half she'd been enrolled at Independent High School, a large suburban high school. Independent sat in the center of a large, green field, surrounded by each of the school's many sports' fields: lacrosse, football, baseball, and soccer. Independent School was known in the area to turn out future sports stars. For this reason, many families tried to get their kids into Independent.

The population at Independent School was not very diverse. Almost everyone was rich and white. Most of the students at the school came from the surrounding suburbs. They came from two-parent homes; most families made six figures. It was definitely an entitled population with an active parent population. There were a few special education students, but most of the high-needs students in the district went to the other high school in town where they were better equipped to handle such needs. As a result, most of the special needs at Independent were relatively mild and easy to accommodate.

Chapter 3

Although Independent was in the suburbs, a large city was just a few miles away. Independent reserved about one hundred spots each year for city kids to be bussed into the school as part of an agreement between Independent's district and the city district.

Hana, a sophomore, was one of these "city kids." She came from a single-family home; her mom worked as a secretary at a city high school, but she struggled to make ends meet. Hana, a sophomore, played lacrosse for the school's team, and she was already hopeful for a college scholarship.

Hana was known as a "good student." She had never been in trouble, and made straight As and Bs. The thing that stood out about Hana was that she had a degenerative eye condition called macular degeneration; Hana was slowly losing her eyesight as she got older. She was rather shy about the condition, but her mom was a wonderful advocate. She had brought several copies of Hana's IEP when she had enrolled her. Independent had only one part-time special education teacher, Miss Tanner, in the building, and she was swamped. It was hard for her to keep up with the paperwork and the needs of her twenty-five students.

Despite Hana's eye condition, she was very bright. She had scored highly on her pre-ACT test, as well as all of her state tests. Hana had the ability to solve complex problems and look at every angle of a situation. She persevered above her disability and was already starting for the varsity lacrosse team as a sophomore. Mr. Gregory couldn't imagine what the problem was or why she was in his office.

Before Hana could say anything, Mr. Welch, Hana's second-hour chemistry teacher, called, clearly enraged. "I'm sending Hana down to your office now," he had snapped. Before Mr. Gregory could ask any follow-up questions, Mr. Welch had hung up.

Mr. Gregory looked up at Hana and gestured to a stiff plastic chair across from him at his desk. She slumped down, her plaid skirt swishing as she moved, and her blond hair hiding her eyes. Despite her obvious intelligence and athletic ability, she was still a teenager.

"What's going on Hana?" Mr. Gregory asked. At this, Hana erupted in tears. He handed her a tissue. After a few minutes, she was able to calm down enough to explain that she had been kicked out of Mr. Welch's class. "But why?" Mr. Gregory asked. Hana just shrugged. Getting nowhere, Mr. Gregory let Hana sit in his office for the remaining five minutes of class. When the bell rang for the next class, Mr. Gregory headed down to Mr. Welch's classroom.

Mr. Welch sat behind his desk grading papers. He was a younger teacher, late twenties at most. He'd been teaching at Independent High School since graduating college five years prior. He'd actually been a student at Independent School himself ten years ago. Mr. Gregory, who'd been at Independent School for fifteen years, remembered him as a student: smart and serious.

Unlike most of the students at Independent, Mr. Welch had not had an athletic bone in his body.

Mr. Gregory asked Mr. Welch what was going on with Hana. Mr. Welch looked up from his paper and put his pen down. He went on to explain how Hana didn't do anything in his class. She always just sat slumped in a chair. She refused to work on in-class work and never paid attention to the class lectures unless it was a class discussion. She didn't try on tests and was not putting much of an effort in. This did not sound like the Hana Mr. Gregory knew. Mr. Gregory decided to observe Hana in class the next day to get to the bottom of the situation.

The next day Mr. Gregory sat at the back of the room. He watched as Hana did, indeed, slump in. The chemistry classroom was fairly normal for a high school classroom. Mr. Welch was not a flowery person, so the decorations were very practical: a periodic table and a few diagrams on the wall. In the front, on a large white board, Mr. Welch had written the opening question about where we see chemical reactions in our everyday lives. It was scrawled across the board in rather small, black print. All of the students, except for Hana, got out their notebooks and began responding to the question.

Next to the opening question, there was a clearly stated objective with the accompanying standard written next to it. Everything was straightforward and to the point in Mr. Welch's class.

After five minutes, Mr. Welch called the students together and asked them to stop writing. Again, Hana had never even started the opening question, but when he read the question out loud, she raised her hand to answer. Mr. Welch called on her to answer, and Hana answered correctly. She seemed to brighten up after this, but a few minutes later, Mr. Welch turned on the projector and asked all of the students to keep their notebooks out and begin writing notes about chemical reactions. Again, Hana did not do this. While the rest of the students scribbled away, she sat picking at her nails. However, if Mr. Welch would ask a question, she'd raise her hand to answer. Again, each time she was correct.

After a twenty-minute lecture, Mr. Welch broke the class up into small lab groups. Each group had three students. They got their protective eye goggles on and began working on a simple experiment involving baking soda and vinegar. Hana was working with one other boy in her class. She was the materials manager for her group and had no problem gathering the needed materials. Each group's members had clearly defined roles, which had been explained to them. Mr. Gregory knew from previous observations that Mr. Welch kept the lab groups the same for three months. Each month he changed the roles of the group members: one was a material gatherer, one was a writer, and one was an orator. The orator for Hana's group was apparently absent this day.

Mr. Welch's class operated like a well-oiled machine. His students knew what to expect and when to expect it. His manner was mild, but consistent. He'd clearly been through lab expectations before, and what to expect was not a surprise. The voices grew louder as kids went through the experiment, which was to add water first to baking soda and then vinegar. Obviously, when the vinegar was added, the groups were rewarded with a bubbly explosion.

Because Mr. Welch had such excellent classroom management and always combined experiments with his lectures, Mr. Gregory had always been pleased by his teaching. However, he was starting to see where he was going wrong with Hana.

When the class came back together as a group, Mr. Gregory asked the orators for each group to tell the class what they observed. Because the orator from Hana's group was absent, she took the role. When it was Hana's turn, her eyes lit up and she became quite animated as she described the small explosion that had taken place.

Mr. Welch then handed the students a piece of paper. At the top, it asked students to describe the chemical reaction they saw take place and how it related to some of the things they were discussing in class. Again, Hana did not pick up her pencil and did not turn in the assignment.

Mr. Gregory knew immediately what was wrong.

Instead of discussing with Mr. Welch, Mr. Gregory went to Miss Tanner, Hana's special education teacher. Miss Tanner, as usual, was busy, but he asked her if he could see a copy of Hana's IEP. Miss Tanner gave it to him. "Is there a problem with Hana?" she asked.

"No, it is not Hana; it is Hana's teacher that needs to read the IEP."

Questions for Discussion

1. What can Mr. Gregory do to ensure that all teachers at his school are reading and understanding the IEPs better?
2. What do you think about how Mr. Gregory got to the bottom of the situation? Do you agree with his tactics? Why or why not?
3. How can Independent High School address students with IEPs better given its limited resources?
4. Have you ever had a student like Hana? If so, how did you facilitate a relationship? What did you do to help her succeed? If not, what else could Mr. Gregory do to help Hana?
5. How should Mr. Gregory follow up with the situation?
6. Do you think Hana's parents should be notified about the situation? Why or why not?

CASE STUDY 3.2
A PICTURE OF EQUITY

Standards 4.d and 5.f

Topic: Suburban high school. This case is about helping a teacher realize what she is doing unconsciously. A school leader faces issues of gender equity in the classroom.

Mrs. Cate entered Mr. Shorter's advanced placement calculus class and sat near the back of the room to begin an observation. Instead of pulling out a notebook, she set up her iPad to record the classroom and the instruction. Then she sat back to observe while the iPad did the work of "making note" of the lesson and the interactions between Mr. Shorter and his students.

Mrs. Cate had been the principal of Gran Vista High School for three years, after serving for eight years as an assistant principal. Gran Vista had a student body of 2,300 students and served an affluent suburb of a nearby metropolis. The students were diverse, including 60 percent white, 20 percent African American, 15 percent Asian, and 5 percent Hispanic. The students, most of whose parents worked in the technology industry or at the nearby university, were overall affluent. Only 10 percent of the students qualified for the free or reduced lunch program. The parents of Gran Vista's students had high expectations for the school. They expected students to engage in rigorous, advanced courses that would open doors for them at the country's best universities.

In Mrs. Cate's opinion, Gran Vista's instructional and extracurricular programs were second to none. The school offered at least twenty advanced placement courses on campus each year, and students could also participate in dual enrollment options at the nearby university. If students were interested in a course that was not typically offered, virtual learning opportunities were also available. One student, for example, had taken Mandarin Chinese online the previous year.

Because of the affluent nature of the community and the healthy tax base, Gran Vista High had been blessed with an abundance of technology. Each teacher had an iPad for use in instruction. One of the ways that the faculty used the iPads was to video lessons. Mrs. Cate and the other administrators also used technology to record lessons during their observations. The faculty had responded well, and Mrs. Cate had observed that having the video to reference made post-observation conferences much easier. She had even begun to play portions of the video during the conference so that she could discuss the lesson with the teacher as they talked about how to improve.

So, Mr. Shorter was unfazed by the iPad that Mrs. Cate set up to record him. He continued with the lesson as planned. The students were using their knowledge of calculus to complete a real-world application problem. Groups of students were working to plot a course for a space shuttle, and then also finding the derivatives of the equation that corresponded to their course. Mr. Shorter was circulating among the groups to ask questions that would move the students along in their thinking. Mrs. Cate leaned forward and tried to follow the thought process of the group closest to her. Then she began to focus her attention on Mr. Shorter's interactions with the groups and how he provided scaffolding to the students as they engaged in the higher-level math task.

Mr. Shorter stopped at a group of four young men. He paused to listen to them for a minute, and then he asked them to look at their work to find a calculation mistake. He praised the boys for their work so far and told them they were on the right track. Mr. Shorter then moved to a group of four students—two girls and two boys. One of the girls, Melissa, spoke up and explained the group's thinking so far, but explained that the group was stuck on how to finish the calculation that they had started. Mr. Shorter looked at their work, and then he addressed one of the boys in the group, Thomas: "Thomas, I know that you know how to do this. Can you find where Melissa has made the mistake? Melissa, that was a good try. Let Thomas show you how to correct your work." Melissa handed the paper to Thomas, and the group waited for Thomas to identify the mistake.

Mr. Shorter then moved to the next group, made up of three girls. The group had finished plotting a course for the space shuttle, and they were working on the derivatives. Mr. Shorter paused to look over their shoulders at their work. "Well, I am shocked, ladies!" he said. "You have plotted a course for the shuttle that is correct. It's a pretty easy course—probably the easiest way that you could have used to solve this problem—but it is correct." The girls turned to look at him smiling.

Then, he added, "Did you guys get Jason to help you?" Jason was sitting with the next group, and he had his back to the girls. Anna, one of the girls, looked over at Jason and frowned. "No, he didn't. Why would we need Jason to help us? He's not in our group."

Mr. Shorter smiled at her. "I just know that this math is easy for Jason, and I wondered if he had given you any tips to help you solve this quickly." Mr. Shorter moved away from the group.

Mrs. Cate sat back with a puzzled look. She felt like she was noticing a trend in the classroom that she didn't like, but she wasn't sure. She decided to remain in the classroom for longer than usual to continue observing the interactions between Mr. Shorter and his students. The groups finished their task, and Mr. Shorter called the class back together so that they could discuss the task. "This was a difficult one," Mr. Shorter said. "But, I am proud of how some of you worked the problem using your knowledge of calculus.

Thomas, could you come up and explain how your group worked to solve the problem?"

Thomas stood up to move toward the front. "Hey, Melissa," he said, "Can I borrow your notebook so I can see where you wrote down what our group did?" Melissa handed her notebook to Thomas, and Thomas copied the work onto the whiteboard for the class to see. "Excellent, Thomas," Mr. Shorter praised. "This was a great way to plot a course for the shuttle. Okay, next let's have Jason come up and show how his group worked the problem." Jason moved to the front of the room and wrote down what his group had calculated. Anna raised her hand.

"Mr. Shorter," Anna said, "I think Jason has made a mistake in the second line of the problem. There should be a negative in front of that five, right?"

Mr. Shorter stepped back to look at the problem. "Jason," he laughed. "You were so busy getting to a brilliant answer that you forgot a negative. Not to worry; I know what you meant. Alright, class, let's move on to our notes for today."

"Mr. Shorter," Anna called. "What about our group—are we going to be able to share our solution?"

"Not today, Anna, dear," Mr. Shorter replied. "I think we've seen the two most complex solutions that were developed in class today, and your group's solution was the more simplistic way to solve the problem." Mr. Shorter erased the solutions from the board and began writing a new problem for students to copy into their notes.

Mrs. Cate stopped the recording on her iPad and rose to leave the classroom. She smiled at Anna as she passed her desk and gave her a thumbs up. Anna smiled back.

That afternoon, Mr. Shorter came to Mrs. Cate's office to discuss the observation. Mrs. Cate smiled as he walked in and sat down. "Mr. Shorter, I want us to watch some of the lesson that I recorded today." Mrs. Cate walked around her desk to take a seat next to Mr. Shorter. "First, let me say that I really liked this activity," Mrs. Cate said. "This is the type of real-world application of skills that will prepare our students for college and then their careers."

Mr. Shorter nodded. "Yes, I agree. I try to incorporate activities like this into the classroom, but they are difficult for some of the students who probably aren't going into the math or science fields."

Mrs. Cate smiled, "Yes, but this type of critical thinking will prepare them well for anything they do in life—whether it involves calculus or not. Let's take a look at the video."

Mrs. Cate started the video at the point when Mr. Shorter began moving from group to group. She watched his face as he viewed his interactions with the groups—first the group of boys, second the group of boys and girls, and third the group of girls. Mrs. Cate then stopped the video. "What do you notice about this part of the lesson?"

Mr. Shorter shrugged. "I was actually surprised that the first group did not already have an answer for me. Those boys are super smart. Aidan's father is a math professor at the university, and Depak's father works for a tech development firm in the city."

Mrs. Cate furrowed her brows. "What do you notice about your interactions with the students in the video? Let me start—I noticed that only one group did have an answer when you rotated to them—Anna's group."

Mr. Shorter smiled. "Yes, they did, didn't they? I was surprised by that. I didn't think those three girls had it in them. But, I guess they did choose a simplistic way to solve the problem, so they got an answer first."

Mrs. Cate leaned toward Mr. Shorter. "I saw something different. Sometimes the simplest path is the best. I thought they did a great job of plotting a simple trajectory for the space shuttle."

Mr. Shorter looked back at the video screen thoughtfully. "I guess I didn't think of that."

Mrs. Cate continued, "I also noticed that when they showed you their answer, you asked them if Jason had helped them. Why did you do that?"

Mr. Shorter looked at Mrs. Cate. "Well, I guess because they surprised me. I didn't expect them to be able to do the problem, and I just assumed they had gotten a smarter student to help them."

Mrs. Cate raised her eyebrows. "Mr. Shorter," she said, evenly. "Why would you think that Jason is smarter than those three girls? Do you realize that Anna is first in the senior class—ranked higher than all of her peers? Courtney, who was also in her group, has the highest SAT score in the class—she made a perfect score on all three sections."

Mr. Shorter looked at Mrs. Cate in astonishment. "No way!"

Mrs. Cate shook her head. "Yes, it's true. Also, if you are impressed by who the students' parents are, Melissa—who asked you a question and you told her to get Thomas to help her—is the daughter of two scientists who work for NASA."

Mr. Shorter sat back in astonishment. "I didn't know that."

Mrs. Cate turned off the iPad. "Mr. Shorter, I am glad that I recorded this lesson, but I am disappointed that you did not see the pattern that I saw. Throughout the lesson, it was very apparent that you favored the male students—praising them, even when they made mistakes. You were dismissive of your female students—even when they had the right answers."

Mr. Shorter shook his head. "I did not mean to do that. I would never intentionally treat my students unequally."

Mrs. Cate nodded. "I believe you, but the fact is that you did, and even when you watched the video back, you didn't pick up on the fact that you were doing it. I want us to meet again tomorrow to review this video again. I want you to reflect tonight on your perceptions of your students—male and female—and be honest about how you arrived at those perceptions. I want you to think about who you see when you look at your students. What are your hopes for their futures? And, if you see something different or have different aspirations for them just based on gender, then you need to stop and begin to question why."

Mr. Shorter nodded. "I can do that. I will do that."

Questions for Discussion

1. Think about how Mrs. Cate uses technology as part of the observation. What do you think about this? What are the pros and cons of an administrator using technology to record a lesson as part of an observation?
2. Describe the specific things that Mr. Shorter does that creates gender inequality in his classroom.
3. Even when Mrs. Cate played the video back for Mr. Shorter, he did not recognize that he had treated the students differently. Describe how you would, as an administrator, help a teacher to see an issue in their classroom that they seem "blind" to.
4. Discuss how Mrs. Cate addressed her concerns with Mr. Shorter after the observation. Would you have addressed the concerns in a similar manner? What would you have done differently?
5. How can a school be proactive in addressing issues of inequality based on gender, ethnicity, or other factors?

CASE STUDY 3.3
SPECIAL EDUCATION TEACHING CO-TEACHING

Standard 4.a and 4.c.

Topic: Suburban middle school. This is a grade six language arts lesson on citing textual evidence with co-teaching as a model, showing the issues that arise in creating effective co-teaching strategies.

Only two weeks into the school year, Ms. Greeley was really looking forward to her first observation of the year. She was observing Mrs. Finely, the new special education teacher, and Mr. Garp, a sixth-grade language arts teacher. Mrs. Finley had been hired in August with the hopes that the special education program would turn around a bit at Rock Bridge Middle School. The last year at Rock Bridge had been rocky within the special education department.

Rock Bridge was in an affluent part of a small city in the Midwest. The school was located in the suburbs. More than 90 percent of the students at Rock Bridge were Caucasian, and the school had very little diversity, including when it came to special education.

Unlike some of the other schools Ms. Greeley had worked at, Rock Bridge's parents were very active in the school. The parent-teacher association was considered to be an elite club. On days when parents were invited in the building (parent-teacher conferences, fund-raisers, concerts, etc.), the building was packed. For the most part, this was a great thing. Who doesn't want active parents in a school? However, this meant the faculty had to be on their game. Every "I" had to be dotted, and every "T" had to be crossed because parents were always looking for some mistake.

The parents at Rock Bridge were well-educated and wealthy. About 25 percent of the households at Rock Bridge had at least one parent who stayed at home, so this gave them time to ensure that things were going well at the school. *Maybe a little too much time*, Ms. Greeley thought begrudgingly.

Last year, the school had gotten the district's attention when it came to special education. It had always been a bit of an afterthought at Rock Bridge. With only twenty-eight students in the school with special needs, the school had just two special education teachers. All of these students were mainstreamed (in the regular classrooms). The district allocated resources so that students with higher needs were bussed to the other middle school in town. The special education teachers at Rock Bridge were asked to stay in compliance with the special education laws, but it wasn't a program they gave much attention to. This was until Penny Price showed up with her son Mark. Penny was a prominent member of the parent-teacher association and was very active in the school; her son was also autistic and received special education services.

The other special education teacher in the building was an older lady named Ms. Perkins. She was nice and formed good relationships with the students, but Ms. Greeley later found out that her IEPs were sparse at best. They had many missing components, but because most special education students flew under the radar at Rock Bridge, Ms. Greeley and the other administrators did not know about the problems.

The year before, when her son, Mark, was in the sixth grade, Penny Price had claimed that her son's IEP was not being followed, and frankly, it wasn't. Ms. Perkins, then the only special education teacher, had written that Mark needed to be seen for one hour a day in his math class by a special education teacher. Well, that wasn't happening at all. Ms. Perkins, the special education teacher who was supposed to be delivering the minutes to Mark and a few other kids in the class, never showed up in the classroom at all!

They were lucky they didn't get in bigger trouble than they did. Luckily, the school was able to glaze it over and make it look not as bad as it really was to the parents, but action needed to be taken to make Penny happy, and rightfully so. Rock Bridge put Ms. Perkins on a plan to help her and hired another special education teacher, Mrs. Finley. This seemed to appease Penny for the moment, but she was already asking when she could come observe Mark in his classroom, and it was only two weeks into the school year! Ms. Greeley wanted to observe Mrs. Finley herself prior to inviting Penny in, but she knew her ability to hold the mother off had a time limit.

Mrs. Finley was now the department head for special education at Rock Bridge. Her job was to help the other special education teacher, Ms. Perkins, form better working relationships with teachers. Mrs. Finley had been hired because she had more than five years' experience with co-teaching, and this what they really wanted to bring to Rock Bridge. Co-teaching, the act of two teachers working together to deliver the same content, was something that was very important to Ms. Greeley. After the ordeal the year before, she didn't want any more trouble, and she believed that, with a mainstreamed special education population, co-teaching was essential.

After speaking with an anxious Penny in her office a few days prior, Ms. Greeley had arranged with Mrs. Finley a time for her to be observed. However, it wasn't just Mrs. Finley who was being observed; it was Mr. Garp. He had been a language arts teacher at Rock Bridge for seven years. He had started the same year Ms. Greeley had been hired as principal.

In fact, he had been her first hire, and it had been a good one. They'd recruited him straight out of the local college, and he'd served the school well ever since. Mr. Garp was a reliable teacher, his students respected him, and his content was generally differentiated and well delivered. He was also a teacher who was fairly receptive to new ideas, and co-teaching was certainly a new idea at Rock Bridge. Ms. Greeley thought if there was any teacher to observe Mrs. Finley with, it was Mr. Garp. Plus, Penny's son, Mark, was in their class second period.

Ms. Greeley was excited to see what changes had come about. She shoved back from her desk and its mound of never-ending papers and walked down the school's sparkling new wing, which was painted seafoam green. The few kids in the hall, who all had hall passes in their hands, said hello to Ms. Greeley politely.

When Ms. Greeley got to the big metal door of Mr. Garp's classroom, it was right before transition to the next class. Ms. Greeley wanted to see the entire period unfold. After Ms. Greeley settled in her seat at the back of the class (a few kids looked at her nervously), the bell rang, and they filed neatly out of the door. The students had five minutes to transition to classes, and Mrs. Finley showed up in the room with just a minute to spare. The cart she used as a movable desk rattled in; it was decorated in pink trim. Mrs. Finley had various baskets and bins with pencils, highlighters, and other tools on her neatly arranged cart. At the bottom of the cart was a locked cabinet, likely where she kept IEPs.

As the sixth graders settled in, they glanced at the board, where Mr. Garp had written a prompt for them to write in their English notebooks. It was asking them to write about one thing they knew to be true and why they knew that. The objective of the day's lesson was written neatly on the board next to the date. After a brief reminder from Mr. Garp about how to label their notebook pages, it was fairly quiet in the classroom as the students got out their English notebooks and labeled the page with the date and the prompt.

Ms. Greeley noticed that many of the students had no problem copying from the board, but within the seven minutes Mr. Garp gave them to respond to the prompt, many of the special education students (there were five, including Mark, in the class of twenty-nine) didn't do much more. Mrs. Finley walked around and whispered to a few of them.

After the writing prompt time was up, Mr. Garp called on a few students to respond and then went on to introduce the day's lesson: citing textual evidence. At this point, Mrs. Finley had interacted only with her special education students. There was no co-teaching really going on that Ms. Greeley could notice.

At this point, Mrs. Finley helped a couple of the students pass out the text books. Mr. Garp split the kids into groups of five. Mrs. Finley noticed that Mark and the other special education students were lumped together in two of the six groups. The students were asked to read the first two paragraphs of a passage (using either a volunteer to read aloud or reading silently to themselves) and then answer a question about it. They were supposed to put a sticky note where they found the evidence in the text that helped support their answer.

Mr. Garp gave the students ten minutes for this task. Ms. Greeley again noticed the special education students, including Mark, struggling to complete the task. Many of these special education students chose one person in the group to read the text rather than read it independently. However, they did not contribute to the group conversation or try to answer the question.

Mrs. Finley, during this time, walked around the classroom. A few of the special education kids raised their hands and asked her a question, but Ms. Greeley did not see Mrs. Finley interacting with the class as a whole. In a true co-teaching environment, it should be hard to tell who is the subject teacher and who is the special education teacher. That was not what was happening in this case. Ms. Greeley felt herself growing disappointed. Mrs. Finley was acting like a glorified teacher aide. This was not what Ms. Greeley had in mind when she'd hired the new special education teacher.

After ten minutes, Mr. Garp called the class back together and asked for one volunteer from each group to report back to the class what they had found. Again, none of the special education students spoke up. Instead, they slunk in their chairs with defeated looks on their faces.

Rock Bridge had a block schedule, so this particular lesson was an hour and twenty minutes long, perfect for the class to get through the short text. Mr. Garp had the groups work through the text two to three paragraphs at a time.

Each time they had to answer a question in their notebooks about the text, and each time they had to put a sticky note where they found the answer and refer back to this point when they wrote their answers. After an hour of this group work, the class was finished with the text. Still, the special education students seemed to just be copying their peers. They never contributed anything to the groups or the class conversation. Mrs. Finley continued to float around the classroom like an aide.

After finishing the text, Mr. Garp led everyone in a very brief five-minute classroom lecture about the importance of citing text in a written answer. Then Mrs. Finley passed out an exit slip. Ms. Greeley glanced at the exit slip as Mrs. Finley handed her one. It correlated well with the lesson. Students were asked to read four sentences and then answer a question, citing evidence in the text. The last seven minutes of class were given to this activity. Any kids who finished early were encouraged to start their homework (a longer passage and a question). When the bell rang, the sixth-graders filed out of the room, their voices humming.

As the kids were leaving, Ms. Greeley went to Mr. Garp and asked to see the exit slips. She also told Mrs. Finley and Mr. Garp to come to her office together during their planning. The two exchanged nervous glances but agreed. "Can I keep these until then?" Ms. Greeley asked, indicating the exit slips. Mr. Garp nodded.

Back at her office, Ms. Greeley looked at the exit slips. Ms. Greeley liked exit slips because they were a great formative assessment to use and help guide future lessons with. She was glad Mr. Garp had used them. Ms. Greeley chose four to use as an example for the pair of teachers. Two were by special education students, and two were not. The two that were by special education students had sparse answers. One student simply rewrote the question while the other was totally off base; neither cited the text. The two exit slips by non-special education students were a bit better. One, in fact, was perfect. It answered the question and cited text, while the other only answered the question without citing the text.

Ms. Greeley truly felt like there would not be such a gap in the results if the teachers had done a better job co-teaching. Mr. Garp, as the lead teacher, and Mrs. Finley, as the aide, had not been the co-teaching model the school had been after. Instead, the school had wanted two teachers who worked together in such a seamless way that you couldn't tell who was who in the classroom. Ms. Greeley remembered looking at a model of co-teaching in a professional development where it showed the teachers co-teaching in a variety of effective ways: splitting the class into two groups, tag-team teaching, and small group teaching (possibly effective for the lesson she had just witnessed).

But how could Ms. Greeley communicate this to the teachers without making them feel disheartened? She wanted to change the norm for this pair in an encouraging way. After all, the situation wasn't totally surprising. Mr. Garp had been teaching at Rock Bridge for a lot longer than Mrs. Finley. He was probably set in his ways, and from Mrs. Finley's perspective, it was hard to come in as a new teacher and change things. Co-teaching was not easy, and Ms. Greeley wasn't going to get anywhere with them by putting them down or making them feel bad. Instead, she had to lift them up, but how?

When Mrs. Finley and Mrs. Garp came to the office the next day, Ms. Greeley had a lot of questions for the pair.

Questions for Discussion

1. Explain your experience with co-teaching or how you have seen it conducted.
2. List and explain some of the challenges that arise when trying to make an effective co-teaching model.
3. Explain some changes that Ms. Greeley can make school-wide to help change the culture of the school into one that embraces co-teaching.
4. Ms. Greeley is disappointed but is not angry at the teachers or want to berate them. Do you agree with this approach? Why or why not?
5. What would be your next steps if you were the principal? Explain in detail.

CASE STUDY 3.4
WHAT'S IN A NAME: ONE STUDENT'S
TALE OF GENDER IDENTITY

Standards 3.a, 3.g, and 5.a

Topic: Urban high school. This case is about issues centered around gender-specific policies in a school to account for transgender students.

Yolanda was anxious about being admitted to the new charter school from the moment she found out that there were uniforms. Although she'd already had the talk with her mother about "coming out" as gay, transitioning from a biological male to female became a learning experience for both of them. It wasn't until they reached the new charter school that things became even more of a challenge.

Although this high school class was bigger than her middle school classes (with approximately thirty students in contrast to eighteen), she was hoping that a bigger class would mean less attention being paid to her. At her elementary school, she noticed students distancing themselves from her as she grew her hair out, lost weight, and started to wear more fitted clothing, and heard whispers of whether she was gay. Friends became associates and then strangers.

Over the summer, she and her mother moved to a new neighborhood, closer to the zoning area that would allow her to attend this school. Otherwise she would've been stuck at a high school that mirrored the students from her eighth-grade class, and Yolanda had no desire to go through that again.

Freshman year was an opportunity to get away from her memories of eighth grade. She graduated from junior high in a small suburb and hoped that with age comes wisdom, or at least less rumors. But the uniform was going to be a problem, and she knew it.

The school uniform at her high school for all students required a yellow men's dress shirt for boys and a yellow blouse for girls. While both boys and girls were allowed to wear navy pants, girls also had the option of wearing navy blue skirts. Both groups of students could wear dark-colored navy or black shoes.

Although Yolanda was growing her hair out, hints of increasing stubble and a tall stature had already started to creep up on her. Her pronounced cheekbones and broad shoulders were already showing signs of masculine features, regardless of Yolanda toning her jogging hobby down to decrease her genetic muscle toning. That still didn't stop the confused stares on her first day when Yolanda showed up to class with what was considered a girl's uniform: yellow blouse, navy blue skirt, pantyhose, and navy blue ballet flats.

Her teacher, Mrs. Bays, didn't say anything when she came into the classroom, but the look of astonishment wasn't missed by Yolanda. However, whereas Yolanda thought the uniform was going to be the biggest obstacle, she realized there were going to be a host of other issues.

All of Yolanda's eighth-grade school transcripts had her name down as Yusef, the name her mother gave her at birth before the transition. Although her mother had explained to the admissions department to refer to her by Yolanda, none of the official paperwork had this name, and her birth certificate had not been changed. Her mother had been too busy making sure Yolanda got all the necessary immunization shots and making sure her grades were up to par all of the previous year to get into this school. But her mother had assured her that the staff knew what to identify her as.

So on the first day of class, she walked into the classroom with her new name, new outfit, new hair, and new body, and she hoped to have a positive experience at this new school. But by the time attendance was called, she realized she may have been a bit too optimistic.

When her teacher, Mrs. Bays, called out the name Yusef, Yolanda did not answer. The teacher's hand made a marking notion, in the manner someone would use when marking a student as absent. Mrs. Bays stared quizzically at Yolanda but said nothing. Although the teacher called out other students' names and pointed to students who did not raise their hands or say "present" aloud, Mrs. Bays did not inquire about Yolanda. When the teacher finished taking attendance and still didn't acknowledge Yolanda, she pondered on how to notify Mrs. Bays of her name change without bringing even more attention to herself.

Mrs. Bays introduced herself to the class and discussed what supplies would be needed in order to pass the course. The usual talks of tardiness, attendance rates, and school supplies were nothing she hadn't heard before. But Mrs. Bays made a point of mentioning that anytime students did not show up in uniform for first period, she would take away points against their grade. Of course in a school that requires uniforms, that made sense. However, it was the way Mrs. Bays explained the uniform situation that caused Yolanda to raise an eyebrow.

"Your parents should've already told you that uniforms are a requirement in order to attend this school," Mrs. Bays said. "And I don't want to see any funny business either, guys. The boys should be wearing pants, not skirts. What you do on Halloween is up to you, but in this class, we follow the rules."

A few boys chuckled and looked in the direction of Yolanda or whispered jokes under their breath, conspiring to wear a skirt the next day. But Yolanda never laughed. Instead she made direct eye contact with Mrs. Bays, who glanced right back at her before continuing on with the first assignment.

Mrs. Bays walked to the front of the class and started an algebra problem. When she asked a student to come to the board to work out the problem, Yolanda raised her hand. Mrs. Bays met Yolanda's glance again. Without calling Yolanda by name, Mrs. Bays pointed and made a motion with her finger to come to the board.

The finger motion was not what Yolanda had planned. She assumed that Mrs. Bays would then ask for her name or call her by name before allowing her to come to the front of the classroom. Yolanda worked out the problem on the board, signing her name "-Yolanda" at the bottom of the chalkboard to identify herself. If Mrs. Bays wouldn't ask for her name, she'd volunteer it and hopefully rectify the attendance situation, too. Mrs. Bays walked to the board, asking Yolanda to stay there in case any corrections needed to be made.

Yolanda stood to the side of the board, quietly waiting for the results. While Mrs. Bays worked quietly, Yolanda glanced at the teacher's desk. On the attendance roster, the name Yolanda was crossed out with a Sharpie marker with "Yusef" handwritten in place of it. There was a checkmark next to "Present" instead of "Tardy" or "Absent." Although Yolanda had not acknowledged her former name, Mrs. Bays clearly knew who she was.

Mrs. Bays eyed the math problem, told her it was correct, and Yolanda went back to her seat. But instead of acknowledging the name at the bottom of the chalkboard, she erased "Yolanda" and started writing a new math problem in place of it. While some students may have considered it just a way to utilize the full board, Yolanda immediately caught on that there were plenty of places on the board to write a new problem and only her name was erased. This was the second time Mrs. Bays showed signs of refusing to acknowledge her by name.

When volunteers were asked to complete the next math problem, Mrs. Bays called on someone else, ignoring Yolanda's hand raised again. Before the next student was allowed to come to the front of the class, Mrs. Bays asked the student for his name. He stated his name as Roger. She checked the attendance roster to verify the name, repeated it, and motioned for him to come up. Again, Yolanda noticed the difference in the way the two students were acknowledged.

The teacher did not call on Yolanda after that even though Yolanda volunteered every single time the teacher asked a question. Yolanda wasn't sure what to do at this point. She was sure that her mother had filled out all the applications with her new name. She'd even spoken with her mother to make sure that the admissions counselors knew what name she went by. So what was it about Mrs. Bays that made her ignore the name?

Before she could think more of it, Mrs. Bays asked the class to get into groups to work out a new set of math problems. She said whichever group got the most problems correct would receive a treat the next day, but the competition would be boys versus girls. When desk tables were turned to divide the classroom into two, Yolanda wasn't sure which side she should go on. She knew the group she identified with was the girls' side, but she wondered if they would allow her into the group. There was only one way to find out. She turned her desk toward the group of girls, excluding herself.

Mrs. Bays immediately spoke up and told her to go to the boys' group. Before Yolanda could speak up, Mrs. Bays spoke up again.

"There are only thirteen boys in this class and seventeen girls," Mrs. Bays said. "There are too many girls already so you should join in with them."

Yolanda turned and quietly counted the heads of twelve boys. It was obvious that Mrs. Bays considered her the thirteenth male student. Just to be sure, Yolanda turned to count the heads of seventeen girls. The classroom became quiet with twenty-nine pairs of eyes all looking to see what Yolanda would do. She looked from Mrs. Bays to both groups and then asked to go to the restroom. Mrs. Bays told her to hurry back because they only had about twenty minutes left of the fifty-minute class. Yolanda walked out of the classroom and headed to the library instead to hide out until class was over.

Questions for Discussion

1. Who should be held accountable for not referring to Yolanda by her chosen name: the principal who should instruct teachers to do so or is this the responsibility of the teacher? Why is this important?
2. Should the name "Yusef" be removed, although official documentation has her down by that name?
3. If the official documents have the name "Yusef," how will this affect grades for the transcript?
4. Should group assignments between boys and girls be eliminated in a school setting to avoid some students feeling uncomfortable?
5. How should teachers treat Yolanda's choice of school uniform? Should the gender-specific policies change to account for transgender students?

CASE STUDY 3.5
NEVER JUDGE A GENDER BY ITS COVER

Standards 3.c, 3.d, and 5.a

Topic: Urban middle school. This case is about changing for physical education class. The issue arises when modest religious students or gender fluid students are uncomfortable changing in front of their peers.

Ask any eighth grader about school uniforms, and chances are they're going to scowl about them. But in Christian's case, it was a relief. This was one of few moments that she felt like she fit in at school. Everyone wore the same maroon and white outfit, along with the same dark shoes. Girls and guys had the opportunity to wear pants, and she just didn't feel like going through the hassle of wearing a skirt, although it was the uniform she preferred.

In this school, it felt like she knew every student there. Those students knew the secret she'd been trying unsuccessfully to hide since about fourth grade when she first kissed a boy. The "problem" wasn't that she kissed a boy at such a young age. The problem was that she was believed to be a boy kissing another boy in fourth grade. Four years later, and her peers would still remind her of it every now and then, although the teachers had no idea.

Regardless of what her birth certificate said her gender was, Christian considered herself a girl trapped in a boy's body. In her case, "playing like a girl" or "throwing like a girl" wasn't always accurate. Because even "playing like a boy" or "throwing like a boy" didn't add up to what stereotypes would make it believe. An athlete, she was not—and every year in physical education classes, she proved it.

But this year, she'd decided she was going to start embracing herself more. She was determined to change in the locker room that she felt she was more suited to be in: the girls' locker room. For seven years straight, she'd always gone into the boys' locker room and restroom, and she felt awkward in there. She did not want to feel uncomfortable anymore, but she hadn't told her parents, teachers, or even family friends what she was about to do.

She'd been thinking about it all summer long. Even in summer school, she pondered on how she would go about taking that first step. In summer school, she would wait until the end of the day or visit a nearby fast-food restaurant after school was out. However, she knew eventually she would have to visit the school restrooms.

She'd already faked being sick for the past week to avoid having to go into the boys' locker room to change. Physical education classes were unisex so she knew she would have to eventually face her peers in one locker room or the other, and she preferred to go to the locker room that matched her self-identified gender.

Christian knew that not participating in physical education could cause her to fail the course. But Mr. Coleman, her physical education teacher, threw a monkey wrench into the plan that would've bought her some time. He insisted that she wear the physical education uniform even if she sat on the bleachers. Because physical education was after lunch, she would change into her uniform at the nearby restaurant and then walk back toward the school. However, today was one of those autumn days that seemed more like winter, and strolling even one block with maroon shorts, a white T-shirt, and white sneakers was not desirable in today's windy weather that felt like below zero temperatures. Today, she didn't go out for lunch, but she knew she had to suit up.

She ended her lunch earlier than usual and headed to the gymnasium, hoping that there wasn't a class already in there. To her relief, there were only a handful of students left and strolling out in their regular school uniform. She stood around wasting time, hanging close enough to one group hoping the previous physical education teacher wouldn't notice she wasn't in his class. He didn't. Creeping her way toward the girls' locker room after the last girl walked out, she hurriedly changed in a stall and scurried out, dropping her regular uniform into her book bag and leaning it against the lockers, hopefully unseen and easy to grab when class ended.

However, she had to use the restroom too. While in the stall, she plotted on how she would wait until all of the girls left again and then return to the girls' locker room to change back into her own clothes. She'd probably be late to her next class, but it would be worth it. She was confident in her plan.

Unfortunately, that confident smile was wiped off of her face the moment she walked out of the stall to wash her hands and saw three other female classmates. One of them, Deirdre, started screaming.

"Why is this boy in the girls' locker room?" Deirdre shrieked. "Christian, get out of here."

When Christian followed Deirdre's order, Deirdre stalked behind her. "I'm going to tell Mr. Coleman on you."

Mr. Coleman, who was standing on the other side of the gym talking to a few other students, was none the wiser until Deirdre stormed over to him.

"Christian was in the girls' locker room," Deirdre said.

Mr. Coleman looked from Deirdre to Christian for an explanation. Christian avoided eye contact. Finally, Mr. Coleman spoke up.

"Well, why were you in there?" the teacher asked.

"Can I speak to you privately?" Christian muttered.

"No, talk to me now," Mr. Coleman said. "You felt bold enough to go into the girls' locker room like a pervert. Explain yourself."

"Please?" Christian begged.

Deirdre huffed and stormed away, yelling, "If Christian comes back into this locker room again, I'm calling my mother."

The two male students who were talking to Mr. Coleman grinned and got ready to follow Deirdre to find out the full story. Mr. Coleman held them back, ordering them both to get changed before class started. For that brief moment, Christian and Mr. Coleman were by themselves.

"What were you in the girls' locker room for?" the teacher repeated.

"I feel more comfortable in there," Christian mumbled.

"Comfortable in there?" Mr. Coleman shouted back. "Hello! News flash. Have you been paying attention in biology, son?"

Christian opened her mouth to say something else but looked back down when she saw the squinted eyes and curled lipped expression on Mr. Coleman's face. She knew that anything else she said would fall on deaf ears.

"If I find you in the girls' locker room again spying on them, you're out of here," Mr. Coleman threatened. "I don't care what kind of weird stuff you do on your own time. You won't do it in my class."

Christian nodded.

"I do not feel well," she said. "Can I sit on the bleachers today?"

"No," he said. "Since you felt the need to pull these pranks, you're playing dodgeball today. And, son, I can't even save you from the amount of clobbering you'll probably get today. You brought this on yourself."

As Mr. Coleman suspected, that is exactly what happened. From head to toe, students threw dodgeballs at her and her only. By the end of class, she was sore and limping away.

Before Christian could walk away, Mr. Coleman smiled at her and said, "I bet that'll teach you to do that again. Take a bath. You'll be all right."

While Christian held back tears, she remembered that she'd left her uniform and book bag in the girls' locker room after Deirdre's outburst. She knew she'd be forced to either wait until all of the girls left again or risk another dodgeball incident like this tomorrow. Instead of facing him again or the girls, she walked out of the gymnasium and sat on the floor, hoping they would all clear out so she could return for her things. After five minutes or so, her peers all left the gymnasium. But she hadn't seen Mr. Coleman yet.

She opened the door again, ignoring the ring of the bell confirming she was now officially late to her next class, and walked back inside. She rushed into the girls' locker room looking for her bag. All of her belongings had been pulled out of the bag with footprints all over them, including her uniform. Her books and book bag were drenched with what smelled like urine. She tried to brush off some of the footprints and put her dirty uniform back on, knowing it was too cold outside to wear her gym uniform for the rest of the day.

She peeked out of the door again to see if the coast was clear. Mr. Coleman hadn't shown his face again, so she guessed he was in the boys' locker room or she'd missed him. When she walked out of the locker room and crossed to the doors of the gymnasium, she heard someone clear his throat. When she turned around, she saw Mr. Coleman sitting on the bleachers.

"I told you not to go into that locker room again," he shouted. "Get to the principal's office now. I'm not telling you this again. Matter of fact, I'm going with you."

Christian dropped her head in shame and followed Mr. Coleman toward the principal's office with the smell of urine from her bag permeating her nose.

Questions for Discussion

1. How should Mr. Coleman have handled the locker room situation?
2. Would it be necessary to speak to students' parents first or just let Christian go to her specified locker room to change?
3. Why should there be a unisex bathroom as an option?
4. How should the principal handle Mr. Coleman's behavior toward Christian after she entered the girls' locker room?
5. How should the teacher and principal handle the students who damaged Christian's school property? Write a step-by-step action plan.

6. If there is no proof of who damaged Christian's property, should the students be punished as a group?

Chapter Four

Teaching and Learning

CASE STUDY 4.1
POETRY OUT OF MOTION: STUDENT FAVORITES

Standard 4.d

Topic: Suburban middle school. This case is about an English lesson on poetry and classroom management strategies.

Mr. Hughes gulped down the last few sips of his coffee; as usual, he had left it rather too long, and it had gone cold. He shuffled through his lesson preparation notes, trying not to splutter the bitter, black liquid over them. He enjoyed his grade-eight class, most of the students were intelligent, thoughtful, and full of ideas, and he liked to think that his passion for poetry had rubbed off on them. Studying as an English major at university, Mr. Hughes had once fancied himself to become a writer. His head was often filled with images of him producing a published piece of work to his mother for Christmas, but as graduation neared, the thought of being penniless and unsuccessful scared him off the idea and he opted for the security of a middle school teaching job instead.

    He considered himself fortunate to gain a placement in a fairly well-to-do area and not have the enormous behavior issues to battle with that one can sometimes associate with an urban school in a low socioeconomic area. Still, he had to face his own fights with parents who believed their children to be perhaps a little smarter than they actually were. The morning bell sounded, and he took one last glance at his notes on the poem that he had allocated for homework, along with discussion questions, and readied himself for the onslaught of early morning teenagers.

The students filed in, and Mr. Hughes greeted each of them with his best hearty "good morning" and gave the instruction to sit down, get out their books with the completed homework, and have their pens ready to commence the lesson. As the students readied themselves, Mr. Hughes liked to walk around the classroom; he figured that he had a good chance to see who had completed the task before they had a chance to eye their neighbor's answers during the class discussion. As usual, he noticed that Penny, Theo, Otto, and Meg had pages of notes and streaks of highlighter covering the poem.

This group of bright pupils who sat scattered among the front two rows were his favorites. He knew he shouldn't have favorites, but their ongoing diligence and mature discussion just made them so likable. He showered them with praise, awarded them merit points, and moved on to look over the rest of the class. He was pleasantly surprised to see varying amounts of work being produced. Most students had heeded his request to highlight the main language features of the poem and many had added notes in the margins. However, just as common as his top students pleasing him, he also had a group of students who consistently did not complete their homework. Even when Lucy, Joe, Lily, and Kyle did complete their work, it was riddled with spelling and grammatical errors, and well below the amount he expected. He couldn't figure out why these pupils just didn't pay more attention in class. The bell sounded as the last few books were being opened on desks.

Mr. Hughes took his place at the front of the classroom and proceeded to call the register. He was quickly met with a "yes Sir" by all but one pupil. Freddie Jones was renowned for his tardiness, and it aggravated Mr. Hughes. Freddie was already one of his weaker students, but the fact that he didn't make the effort to show up on time did not sit well with the organized Mr. Hughes.

"Sorry I'm late, Sir," Freddie gasped between gulps of air as he ran in the door. "My alarm clock must be broken; it didn't go off," he added as he took his seat next to Kyle. The class erupted in a fit of giggles. This was a regular excuse for Freddie and was certainly not believed to be the truth. Mr. Hughes marked an "L" for late next to Freddie's name and handed the register to Penny to deliver to school office.

"You always choose Penny," whined Lucy, sending the class into a fit of giggles. Mr. Hughes set about calming the class and began his lesson.

He launched into his lesson, writing the title of the poem on the board. He had given the students the poem "Nothing Gold can Stay" by Robert Frost. They were asked to read the poem for homework, take notes, and answer a few questions. They had been studying poetry long enough that the short, eight-line poem shouldn't have been too difficult. It was one of Mr. Hughes's favorites, particularly for grade-eight students, as the theme of change is so prevalent to them. He always liked the idea of throwing his pupils into the deep end, so to speak. Give them the poem, get their ideas, and go from there. He turned from the board to the class.

"What does this title mean?"

It was both a simple and difficult question. Meg's arm shot straight in the air.

"Yes Meg." Mr. Hughes did not even give anyone else a chance to raise their hand.

"I think it means that all things must come to an end, even special ones."

"An excellent thought, Meg," beamed Mr. Hughes. "Anyone else?"

Otto and Theo both tentatively put up their hands. Mr. Hughes chose Theo.

"Maybe we should appreciate the good stuff because it can disappear before you know it." Theo responded in a less than confident voice.

"Totally!" Mr. Hughes was impressed.

"It's dumb," Lily interrupted. "Isn't gold meant to last forever?"

"Yeah, like my grandma's jewelry!" Kyle joined in. Freddie and Lucy laughed.

"Lily and Kyle!" Mr. Hughes raised his voice. "You make a point Lily, but you must raise your hand before speaking. Can you add more to your answer?"

"No," she said sulkily.

Mr. Hughes decided to move on with the lesson. It wasn't unusual for an interruption to happen so early on, and it always came from that back corner where Lily, Lucy, Joe, Kyle, and Freddie sat. Mr. Hughes continued, trying not to show his annoyance.

"Meg and Theo have both mentioned some good points. Frost is trying to raise the idea that nothing can stay the same forever, and change is bound to happen at some point."

The lesson carried on with a debate about the theme of change. Some students shared Mr. Hughes's idea, some partially agreed, except for a few others who merely thought that Frost was just being rather factual. He called upon answers from Penny and Otto; he noticed out of the corner of his eye that Kyle had raised his hand but decided he couldn't be bothered to deal with a silly answer only to then have to get the class back on track as Kyle would no doubt set them off into another fit of giggles. In a separate glance, he saw that Lucy and Lily appeared to have lost focus, instead drawing pictures on the back page of Lily's notebook.

He couldn't figure out why they just didn't try and participate in class discussions. Granted, they were both not very bright, and their spelling and grammar were atrocious, but every now and again they would offer a reasonable answer. He snapped at them to stop and punished them with a demerit point each. The board at the front of the room was filling up with colorful notes, and a satisfied Mr. Hughes decided to move on with the lesson. Addressing the class, he gave a simple instruction.

"I want you to organize yourselves into groups of three or four and share your notes on the literary terms found in the poem. Make sure you discuss examples."

The class set about shuffling tables and chairs so that they could comfortably face their chosen group, and Mr. Hughes slid his chair from his desk to sit with Otto, Theo, Meg, and Penny. He was keen to hear what his brightest students had come up with, and as usual he was not disappointed. Terms like *alliteration* and *figurative language* filled his ears. The highlighted notes of his students provided accurate examples. Then, out of nowhere a paper dart landed sharply in the middle of the group. Mr. Hughes turned his head swiftly to see Freddie quickly sitting back in his seat, feigning ignorance as he picked up his pen.

"Outside now!" Mr. Hughes was on his feet, finger pointing directly in Freddie's direction. Freddie did not try to argue, instead he rose and left the room as requested, leaving Kyle and Joe behind to stifle their laughter. Mr. Hughes picked up the paper dart, placed it on his desk, and calmed himself. He faced the class and asked them to arrange the desks back to normal in complete silence. The class obeyed, and he was satisfied things were back under control. He began to ask groups for their answers and was given fine examples. Finally, he reached the group at the back.

"All our answers have been said already, sir," Kyle piped up. Mr. Hughes couldn't be sure if this was the truth or a cop out answer. It could very well be true, as Kyle and Joe struggled with English lessons so the chance of them coming up with something that hadn't already been said was highly unlikely.

Mr. Hughes couldn't be bothered to push them further, having had enough of that "back corner" already this lesson. He glanced at the clock and began summing up the lesson, offering praise and merits to Penny and Theo, and explaining that they need to keep their notes for next lesson, when they would be looking at memorizing the poem and how to effectively read it aloud. Mr. Hughes timed his conclusion perfectly, as always, the bell sounding for recess just as he had the students standing behind their desks waiting to be dismissed.

Mr. Hughes stood by the door as the class filed out, but as soon as the last pupil left, he walked straight to his desk and slumped in his chair. He was exhausted. Lily, Lucy, Kyle, Joe, and Freddie, or as he has labeled them, the "troublemakers," could really take it out of him each lesson. He pondered what he could do about the situation as he absentmindedly twirled the paper dart between his fingers and placed it in his top drawer.

As the day progressed, more of the same occurred in Mr. Hughes's lessons. He was repeating the same names over and over so frequently that he was beginning to feel like a broken record. He was thankful to have the second-to-last period free while his class had their music lesson. Mr. Hughes pondered about his "troublemakers" situation. These students didn't seem to be causing the same problems in some of their other classes; in fact, he often received glowing reports from physical education, art, and drama. He concluded that they simply did not want to behave for him. He decided he had enough and to issue detentions to all five.

His students filed back into his classroom, rather animated after their music lesson, and took their seats ready for afternoon role call and notices. Mr. Hughes asked Meg and Otto to hand out the homework folders and handed the list of notices for Theo to read aloud to the class. Meanwhile, Penny was given the whiteboard marker and given the much coveted task of writing pupils names on the board. She had two columns to fill in, one for good behavior and one for poor behavior.

Mr. Hughes would choose a different student each day and award class points to all students with their name in the "good behavior" column. Penny watched the class carefully as they packed their bags and tidied the classroom. Mr. Hughes trusted her and used this time to gather his own belongings together. Upon glancing up, he was surprised to see Lily, Kyle, and Freddie's names in the "good behavior" column and Otto's on the "poor behavior" side. He questioned Penny.

"Lily was the first one packed away, and Kyle and Freddie helped pick up all the small bits of paper off the floor."

"What about Otto?" he asked.

"He was throwing people's homework folders on the desk instead of putting them down gently. Some even fell to the floor." Penny justified herself well. Mr. Hughes just couldn't bring himself to award class points to three of his biggest behavior problems. He overruled.

"Freddie, Kyle, and Lily, after your behavior in English this morning, you will not be issued with class points."

"That's so unfair!" Lily moaned, stamping her foot at the same time.

"The rules are 'If your name gets on the good side, you get class points.' You can't just change it!" Kyle was getting angry.

"My classroom, my rules!" boomed Mr. Hughes.

"But . . ." Freddie began, but was immediately interrupted by Mr. Hughes.

"There are no buts, Freddie. You need to learn there are consequences for your actions. My decision is final!"

That was the end of that. He dismissed the class, who had fallen into complete silence, and slumped at his desk. He opened his top drawer to retrieve his keys; he was desperate to head home. Freddie's paper dart caught his eye, and he noticed that the paper was covered in writing. Curiously he unfolded the paper dart and found a page of Freddie's scrappy writing. At all different angles Freddie had written comments such as "it's not my fawlt i'm dumb," "this work is stupid!" and "it's too hard." It took Mr. Hughes a while to comprehend the messages, the spelling making it hard to understand what each sentence meant. Perhaps he shouldn't be so harsh on Freddie, but if he wasn't, then Freddie would be even more disruptive and the others would just follow suit.

Questions for Discussion

1. Why do you think the "troublemakers" act the way they do in Mr. Hughes' lessons?
2. Why do you think Mr. Hughes doesn't hear reports of negative behavior in other subjects?
3. Instead of getting angry and issuing detentions, how could Mr. Hughes better manage these pupils?
4. Do you think it was right of Mr. Hughes to overrule Penny's "good behavior" column at the end of the lesson? Why didn't he take any action on Otto for being in the "poor behavior" column?
5. What "jobs" could Mr. Hughes give his "troublemakers" to get them involved in class?

CASE STUDY 4.2
CONNECTING WITH THE CONTENT

Standards 5.c and 5.e

Topic: Urban high school. This case is about creating a culturally relevant curriculum and engaging students with curricular content.

Mr. Barksdale walked down the hallway of Holmes High School, on his way to observe new English teacher Candace Elbert. He had been pleased to recruit and hire Ms. Elbert from the job fair at the nearby university last spring. Ms. Elbert wasn't from the city, having been raised in one of the outlying suburbs. However, she had expressed a desire to make a difference in her interview with Mr. Barksdale, and she wanted to go to a place where kids really needed her—needed a caring adult in their lives. Mr. Barksdale had replied that he knew of many kids who needed someone like her at Holmes High School.

Holmes High served 2,100 students in the heart of the city. While Holmes dealt with many of the stereotypical issues of an urban high school, Mr. Barksdale prided himself on the fact that Holmes was a "90/90/90" school. Ninety percent of his students were minority, and ninety percent also qualified for free or reduced price lunch. However, ninety percent of his students passed the state assessments each year.

Mr. Barksdale attributed the success of Holmes High to a laser focus on academically rigorous classrooms, but also on relevant and engaging lessons for the students. His math teachers worked to infuse real-world applications into lessons. His science teachers incorporated hands-on labs and field trips for the students. The nearby university, Ms. Elbert's alma mater, supported the school's efforts tremendously. The university partnered with the school to bring enrichment activities to the students at Holmes, and many college students volunteered as mentors for the Holmes students. In fact, Ms. Elbert had mentored a student at Holmes, which is why she chose to visit Mr. Barksdale's booth at the job fair.

Ms. Elbert had fit right into the culture that Mr. Barksdale had worked to build at Holmes High. She had high expectations for the students, and she really wanted to serve them. Mr. Barksdale was anticipating a great first observation for Ms. Elbert today.

As Mr. Barksdale entered the classroom, he smiled. The focus of the lesson was *Julius Caesar*, the Shakespearian play—definitely a rigorous reading assignment for Holmes's tenth-grade students. Ms. Elbert was at the front of the room, assigning parts to various students in the class. When she was finished, she asked the students to find the appropriate place in the text so that everyone could follow along as the "actors" read their lines. Some of the students groaned as they pulled out their books and found the page, but they all complied. One especially resistant student—whom Mr. Barksdale recognized from countless conversations in his office—did pull out his book when Ms. Elbert stopped by his desk and spoke with him quietly.

Ms. Elbert smiled at Mr. Barksdale as she brought him a book so he could follow along as well. Then she returned to the front of the classroom, and the reading began. The various students read their lines well, and Ms. Elbert had them pause in the reading occasionally so that the class could discuss what they had read. Mr. Barksdale noticed that the "discussion" mainly involved Ms. Elbert explaining what was happening in the play in her own words. At one point, a very outspoken young lady looked at Ms. Elbert and said, "Why don't he just come right out and say that! What you just said! Why does he have to make it so complicated?"

The class laughed, and Ms. Elbert smiled. "In Shakespeare's day, that's how they talked. He's also trying to produce art, so sometimes he will have lines rhyme and he uses figures of speech."

"Ain't no need for that," the girl continued. "Just say it plain. I ain't got time for this!"

"I know it's difficult to understand," Ms. Elbert continued. "But, this is a classic! Whenever someone mentions Shakespeare or Julius Caesar or says 'Et tu, Brutus,' you will know what they mean!"

A young man spoke up, "Nobody around here talks about Shakespeare, Miss, and I promise no one has ever looked at me and said 'Et tu' or anything like that."

The class laughed, as did Ms. Elbert. "At any rate," she replied, "We are going to read this because it's part of our curriculum. So, let's keep going."

After reading several scenes from the play, Ms. Elbert had the students stop reading for the day, and she gave them a graphic organizer to complete on the characters they had met so far in the play. The students were to write down what they knew so far about each character, including lines from the play that supported what they knew. Several students groaned, but Ms. Elbert ensured that they got started on the assignment by circulating around the room. When students struggled, Ms. Elbert helped by pointing them toward key passages in the play that might give them some answers about a specific character.

While the students worked, Mr. Barksdale took notice of the classroom. Ms. Elbert had covered the walls with posters related to literature. She had posters related to the major texts the class would read, as well as posters of famous American authors and famous British authors. Mr. Barksdale recognized many of the authors pictured as writers of the "classics"—Nathanial Hawthorne, Herman Melville, Charles Dickens, Mary Shelley. Mr. Barksdale noticed the daily schedule on the board. Ms. Elbert's tenth-grade classes were reading *Julius Caesar*, and her ninth-grade classes were reading *Romeo and Juliet*.

Mr. Barksdale turned his attention back to the students as they worked on the graphic organizer. Ms. Elbert continued to circulate among the desks, stopping to encourage students or to help them find the information that they needed. Mr. Barksdale was pleased with the way that the students seemed to respond to her—conversing easily with her and complying when she asked them to focus on the task. Yet, Mr. Barksdale was not impressed with the level of engagement of his students with the assignment. He turned to the student next to him and asked, "So, you guys have been reading *Julius Caesar*. Do you like the play?"

The student shrugged. "Not really," he said. "I mean, no offense, Mr. Barksdale, but it's a play about a bunch of white guys who decide to kill the king. The best part was when he was stabbed. After that, it's pretty lame. Who cares about their political issues and stuff. Ancient Rome don't have anything to do with me."

Mr. Barksdale smiled. "Thank you for being honest," he told the student. The bell rang, and the students moved to leave the classroom. Mr. Barksdale walked out with the young man. "What do you think of Ms. Elbert?"

The young man smiled. "She's pretty cool. She's nice to us, but she doesn't put up with our mess. You have to pay attention in there, and everyone respects her because she respects us back. She doesn't talk down to us.

We like her—even if her class is kind of boring sometimes." Mr. Barksdale smiled as the student turned toward his next class.

Mr. Barksdale asked Ms. Elbert to visit him after school the following afternoon. He began the conversation by praising her for her rapport with the students. "The students here are not easy sometimes, but you have classroom management under control. You seem to have a way with them—a mutual respect has been established."

Ms. Elbert warmed at his praise. "I worked very hard the first week of school to establish the classroom expectations, and I let them participate in that. I wanted them to understand that it's our classroom together—not just my classroom. So, we talked about what they wanted to establish as rules and expectations, and that's what we did. They were big on respect, so we all agreed to respect each other and talked about what that would look like."

Mr. Barksdale nodded and agreed that she had taken the right approach with the students. Then he shifted the focus to his main constructive feedback for Ms. Elbert—the relevance of the curriculum. He shared that he was not sure the students found *Julius Caesar* to be especially relevant to the context of their own lives, and nothing in the lesson seemed designed to make it any more relevant.

"I actually agree that it doesn't seem very relevant to them," admitted Ms. Elbert. "I mean the thing about Shakespeare is that the themes are universal—so it's about betrayal and whether it's ever right to do the wrong thing for the right reasons. But, the kids don't really get the language, and they aren't at all interested in the political struggles in ancient Rome. So, now, I am just trying to get through it as fast as I can so we can be finished with it."

Mr. Barksdale encouraged Ms. Elbert to pause and really think about what she had just said. The themes were universal—had she designed any lessons or activities for students to really think about those universal themes and how they might relate to present-day situations?

Ms. Elbert shrugged and said she had not. Mr. Barksdale told her that instead of trying to get through *Julius Caesar* quickly, that she should perhaps stop reading the play with the students for a day or two and design an activity around some of those universal themes. "My suggestion is that you work to help them connect the text to their lives—make it relevant."

Ms. Elbert agreed that she could do that—she had even seen an activity that had students simulate members of a government and respond to various scenarios that arose that might require them to overthrown the ruler. Students were supposed to reflect on what it would take for them to overthrow the person in power. "Maybe I will do this activity with the kids over the next couple of days."

At the end of the week, Mr. Barksdale saw the young man from Ms. Elbert's class in the hallway, in a heated discussion with the outspoken young lady from the class. As they approached Mr. Barksdale, the young lady looked up at him and asked him to weigh in on their conversation. "Mr. Barksdale, don't you agree that it would be okay for us to revolt and overthrow our teacher if she was being unfair and discriminating against certain students?" Mr. Barksdale shook his head smiling. Obviously, Ms. Elbert had gotten the students to think about the themes from *Julius Caesar* in a very relevant way.

Questions for Discussion

1. What positive things did Mr. Barksdale notice in Ms. Elbert's classroom? What negative things did he notice?
2. As an administrator, would it be important to you for teachers to build rapport with students? Explain why or why not.
3. Ms. Elbert built a system of expectations for the classroom with the students' involvement. Do you agree with her strategy? As her administrator, what feedback would you give her on this?
4. What do you think of how Mr. Barksdale handled the issue of culturally relevant curriculum with Ms. Elbert? What other suggestions might you have for her?
5. What do you think of Mr. Barksdale seeking the opinion of a student during the observation? As an administrator, how much stock would you put in what students think of a teacher?
6. What other suggestions would you have for Ms. Elbert as a new teacher?

CASE STUDY 4.3
READY FOR ANYTHING

Standards 4.a and 4.c

Topic: Rural elementary school. This case is about the importance of understanding emergency protocol and procedures.

Mr. Cannon had been the principal of Fortson Elementary for ten years. He enjoyed his job, and he took it very seriously. There was nothing more valuable that the community, and its parents could trust him with than their children. Mr. Cannon worked hard to ensure that the teachers he hired were well-trained and safe to be around his students. He worked hard to train them and impress upon them the huge responsibility that they held when they were responsible for a classroom full of young charges. Mr. Cannon also went over emergency procedures every fall in faculty meetings, and drills were held every month to ensure that teachers and students got to practice. Mr. Cannon wanted his teachers to be ready for anything.

Fortson Elementary School served 440 students in a rural community. The school sat back from the road in a large field. As in most rural communities, many of Fortson's students qualified for free or reduced price lunch—just over 60 percent of them. The community, though, was prideful, and Mr. Cannon often had to have private conversations with parents to convince them that they should take the assistance offered through the school lunch program. Fortson's students were 75 percent white, 15 percent black, 8 percent Hispanic, and 2 percent other.

Mr. Cannon headed to second grade to observe a second-year teacher, Ms. Tyner. Ms. Tyner had done well during her first year, and she was more confident in her abilities this year. As Mr. Cannon entered the room, he noticed that the students were in guided reading groups or centers, and Ms. Tyner was working with one group at a small table. Mr. Cannon sat down and began scripting notes. Ms. Tyner was working with her small group on a guided reading book about a squirrel. As the students participated in choral reading, Ms. Tyner modeled correct pacing and prosody for the students. They paused after a few pages, and Ms. Tyner asked the students several comprehension questions about what they had just read.

Mr. Cannon made note of what the other students were doing. One of the groups was gathered around a large sheet of paper on the floor, and they had their books open. They were drawing a scene from the book that they were reading, and the students were using the book to make sure they had the details in the picture right. "No," one student, Russell, said to the rest of the group. "It says that it was almost night, so we don't need to draw a big sun in the sky. It needs to look like it is almost night."

Another group was gathered around a junior Scrabble game in one of the centers. They were playing Scrabble and building words with word tiles. A final group of students was seated in one corner, working independently on tablets. It looked as if they were using one of the online reading programs that the school had purchased for classroom use.

After another ten minutes passed, Ms. Tyner rang a small bell on the table and asked the groups to move. Like clockwork, the students cleaned up their area and moved to the next station or center. The group that had been with Ms. Tyner moved to the "art" station where they got paper and began discussing the drawing of a scene from their book about the squirrel. The students at the art center moved to the Scrabble game, and those students moved to the tablets. The students who were working on the tablets moved to the table with Ms. Tyner.

Mr. Cannon made note of the smooth transition that the students made from one group to the next. He also made note of the interactions between Ms. Tyner and students and between the students themselves. Ms. Tyner's tone was upbeat and positive, as she scaffolded the reading lesson for the students. The students took turns at their stations and responded to each other by listening attentively and by taking turns. Mr. Cannon noted "Group Rules" posted in a colorful chart on the wall. He smiled at the ones that said "Take turns" and "Don't talk over each other." Mr. Cannon continued to watch as the students rotated one more time, and he began to gather his things to exit the room.

Just then, the fire alarm rang. Ms. Tyner was so startled that she jumped, and then she jumped up from the table, "Ok, students, don't panic. It's probably just another drill. Let's get lined up at the door and I will find my emergency folder." The students clumsily shoved their chairs in and went to line up at the classroom's outside exit door. Mr. Cannon noticed that some of the students engaged in pushing and shoving or arguing about who was in front of whom in the line. Ms. Tyner was frantically rummaging through folders on her desk and then in a file cabinet drawer as she searched for her emergency folder.

Mr. Cannon, who did know that this was a drill, stood and said, "Ms. Tyner, let's concentrate on getting the students outside, and then we will worry about your emergency folder."

Ms. Tyner looked up, flustered. "Of course, Mr. Cannon. Okay, boys and girls, let's go outside." The student at the front of the line opened the door, and the class exited. Mr. Cannon decided to go with them. He watched as the students ran toward where the other classes were gathered, and Ms. Tyner followed behind them. When Ms. Tyner arrived at the designated location, she began to try to gather her students together.

"Boys and girls, I need for us to make a line right here together so that I can see who is here." It took Ms. Tyner several minutes to get all of the students back together, as they had begun to mingle with the other classes of students.

Once she got them together, she started counting the students to ensure that everyone had made it out of the classroom. The students stayed still long enough for her to count them, but then they began to talk among themselves and move around. Mr. Cannon observed that the students in the other second-grade classes remained in their lines, as their teachers moved back and forth from the front to the back of the line to redirect any students who began to move around. Ms. Tyner did not move up or down the line of students. Instead, she began telling one of the other teachers about how she couldn't find her emergency folder and that she did not know where it was.

Mr. Cannon called the front office on his radio and told them to sound the "all clear" for the students and teachers to return to the classroom. Mr. Cannon moved with Ms. Tyner's class back to the classroom. The students were chatting and could not seem to settle down when they reentered the classroom. Ms. Tyner walked over to the table and rang the little bell. The students immediately stopped what they were doing and looked at her for instructions. "Class, I understand that the fire drill was exciting, but now we need to get back to our work. I will count to five while you move back to your groups and pick up where we left off. 1 ... 2 ... 3 ... 4 ... 5 ..."

Mr. Cannon watched as the students moved back to their groups and were back on task within five seconds. He exited the room with a thoughtful expression on his face.

Ms. Tyner came to see Mr. Cannon after school that day to discuss the observation. She looked at him sheepishly when she entered his office. "I am so sorry about the drill," she began. "I did find my emergency folder in the top desk drawer, right where I put it. I just got so flustered today."

Mr. Cannon smiled as he asked Ms. Tyner to sit down. "First, everyone gets flustered now and then. That's why we do these drills—so that you can practice and hopefully not be flustered during an actual emergency. Let's start with your guided reading lesson, though. Your students transitioned so well between the stations. How did you get them to do that?"

Questions for Discussion

1. What positive things were happening during Ms. Tyner's guided reading lesson? Did you notice anything you would ask her to improve about this lesson?
2. What things went wrong for Ms. Tyner and her students during the drill? Did you notice any positives during the drill? Make a list of the things that Ms. Tyner's class needs to improve upon before the next drill.
3. What do you think about how Mr. Cannon handled sharing his concerns with Ms. Tyner? What would you do differently?
4. Should Mr. Cannon count the "drill" as part of his official observation of Ms. Tyner? Is it fair for an administrator to document classroom observations during emergencies or times when the class or teacher is out of the normal routine?
5. Ms. Tyner was very concerned that she could not find her emergency folder, but Mr. Cannon told her to focus on getting the students out of the building. Which is more important during an emergency situation?

CASE STUDY 4.4
WELCOMING EVERYONE

Standards 3.g and 3.h

Topic: Rural high school. This case is about teachers understanding the abilities of their English language learners (ELL). Some ELL students struggle toward comprehending basic material in the classroom, therefore the teacher needs to differentiate instruction.

Mr. Kraus hummed as he walked down the hallway of Overton High School. He smiled and acknowledged students as they passed, asking some about their families and congratulating others on their performance at the baseball game and soccer game from the previous evening. Mr. Kraus had lived in Overton for his entire life. He graduated from Overton High School and returned to teach at the school after a stint in the military and earning his teaching degree. He knew the community, and many of his students were the children of old high school friends.

Overton was growing, however. A new industrial complex on the edge of town, closer to the city, had brought jobs to the area, and contractors had quickly built affordable housing on the outskirts of Overton to handle the influx of workers. Overton High School had welcomed fifty new students in the fall, thirty of whom were Latinx students whose first language was not English. For a rural high school of just over one thousand students, this was big news.

Prior to this year, Overton High had not had an ELL population, so this was a new opportunity and challenge for the faculty. Mr. Kraus had worked to hire a part-time ELL teacher who provided direct services to the students for one period a day, but the students attended regular academic and elective classes for the remainder of the day. Mr. Kraus had focused professional learning activities for this year on how to serve ELL students in the regular classroom. Teachers had attended only one session so far, during preplanning. The faculty, overall, was receptive to the new students and eager to learn about how to best serve them.

Mr. Kraus entered Dr. Burris's biology classroom and took a seat near the back for a formal observation. Dr. Burris was a veteran teacher at Overton. Because of the size of the school, Dr. Burris was one of only two biology teachers. The other teacher, Ms. King, was in her second year of teaching, so Mr. Kraus had decided to cluster the ELL students who needed biology into Dr. Burris's class. Today, Dr. Burris was introducing cells—plant and animal—to the students. When Mr. Kraus entered the room, Dr. Burris was projecting a picture of both a plant cell and an animal cell, and he verbally instructed students to journal about the differences that they noticed between the two.

Mr. Kraus opened his notebook and began to script notes. Dr. Burris moved around the room, returning papers and taking attendance as the students journaled about the two cells. Mr. Kraus noticed that the three ELL students in the classroom were seated in the last row of the classroom. They all three had notebooks open on their desks. One appeared to be writing, one was looking around the classroom at the other students, and the third was holding her pencil, but looking down at her lap.

Mr. Kraus made note of the interactions between Dr. Burris and the students. Dr. Burris moved among the desks, speaking to various students about the graded papers or about the upcoming science fair. He asked two students about the soccer game the previous evening. When he went down the last row, he did not speak to or make eye contact with any of the three ELL students.

After giving the students approximately ten minutes to write about the differences between the cells, Dr. Burris began a class discussion of the noted differences. Students raised their hands and pointed out differences in the structures inside the cells and their shapes. One student wondered if the color of the pictures was accurate or if it made a difference at all. Another student wondered if the plant cell was green because most plants are green. Mr. Kraus made note of the interactions as Dr. Burris called on various students whose hands were raised. The three ELL students did not raise their hands. Two of them watched the other students as the discussion progressed, looking, with interest, at the students who were talking. The third student continued to look down at her lap.

At the end of the discussion, Dr. Burris verbally asked the class to take notes on the plant and animal cells. Dr. Burris projected a t-chart and asked the students to draw the same graphic organizer in their notes. Then he put the picture of the animal cell back on the screen and began to point out characteristics of the animal cell to the students. He asked students to add animal cell characteristics to the left side of their t-chart.

Then he projected the picture of the plant cell and asked students to add plant cell characteristics to the right side of the t-chart. As Dr. Burris lectured, he pointed out various structures of the cells—cell wall, cell membrane, mitochondria, chloroplasts, nucleus, Golgi bodies, cytoplasm, and so on. Mr. Kraus attempted to script the discussion into his notes, but he smiled as he struggled to spell many of the terms.

After the discussion of differences in the two types of cells, Dr. Burris passed out a cell vocabulary worksheet. On it was a list of many of the terms that had just come up in the conversation about animal and plant cells. Dr. Burris verbally instructed the class to use their textbooks to look up the words and write the definitions on the worksheet. The students complied, and

Dr. Burris moved up and down the rows of the classroom to prompt students and make sure they were getting started. He paused beside one student who was asking a question about how plant cells make food from sunlight, and he said the class would get into this information tomorrow. He did point out where the student could read about photosynthesis in the textbook.

Mr. Kraus noted that Dr. Burris, again, did not interact with the three ELL students. All three students took the worksheet. One of the students watched the girl beside him, and he mimicked her actions. He took out his textbook when she did. He opened it to the glossary when she did, and when she began to write down information from the glossary, he did the same. The second student began to write on his worksheet, but he did not have his textbook out. Mr. Kraus could not see what he was writing. The third student took the worksheet, but continued not to engage in the lesson. She was looking down, still, at her lap.

After forty-five minutes of observing in the classroom, Mr. Kraus moved to leave the classroom. He realized that during the entire observation, no one in the classroom had spoken to the three ELL students. While one seemed to try to engage in the lesson, the second one appeared to be putting on a show of being engaged, and the third had never looked up from her lap. Mr. Kraus frowned. While he knew that he was not expert enough to say everything that Dr. Burris should have done to instruct the ELL students, he did know that he should have done more to make them feel welcome in the classroom and check for understanding.

That afternoon Dr. Burris came to Mr. Kraus's office for his post-observation conference. Mr. Kraus asked Dr. Burris how he thought the lesson went. Dr. Burris replied that he was trying to use some of the strategies that the faculty had discussed in the ELL professional development. Mr. Kraus raised his eyebrows in surprise as Dr. Burris continued. Dr. Burris discussed the use of the visuals of the cells, as well as the vocabulary worksheet. But that was it.

Dr. Burris nodded. "I am open to changing my teaching. I would like as much help as I can get. I want to do what's best for the students."

Questions for Discussion

1. How has Dr. Burris reacted to having ELL students in his classroom?
2. Describe the strategies that Dr. Burris used. Why did these things not work for his ELL students?
3. What teaching techniques should Mr. Kraus suggest?
4. How does Mr. Krauss address the issue? What do you think of his plan?
5. What other suggestions would you have for Mr. Kraus or how might you handle this situation differently?

6. What else could the school as a whole do to welcome ELL students to Overton High School?
7. What can Dr. Burris do to help the ELL students feel like a part of the classroom?

CASE STUDY 4.5
SUPPORTING THE NEW TEACHER

Standards 3.b and 3.g

Topic: Suburban elementary school. This is about a principal confronted with a new teacher dressing unprofessionally. This case concerns the staff dress code and if it interferes with learning.

Mr. Tucker, principal of Lovejoy Elementary School, is beginning the school year feeling confident about his staff. While he had to replace several retiring teachers, he was able to choose from some very qualified teacher candidates. The three new teachers who have joined his staff come highly recommended and have completed teacher preparation programs at the nearby university. Based on their qualifications and the high praise they received from their professors and teacher mentors, Mr. Tucker does not anticipate having any problem with his newest faculty members. As a week of preplanning draws to a close, Mr. Tucker feels that the new teachers are fitting in nicely. They have their rooms in order, they seem to be getting along with their grade-level teams, and they all seem ready for their first day of school.

On the first day of school, Mr. Tucker begins the day supervising the arrival of buses and the parent drop-off line. One of the new teachers, Ms. Cane, is also on duty in the drop-off lane. A veteran teacher, Mrs. Strain, comes to Mr. Tucker with a frown on her face. "Mr. Tucker," she begins, "have you see Ms. Cane this morning?"

"Yes, I saw her join us for duty a little while ago," Mr. Tucker replied as he waved to an arriving bus driver and students. "Is something wrong?"

"Some of the parents seem to be a little shocked at what she is wearing," explains Mrs. Strain. "It's probably appropriate for her age, and she looks cute, but it's a little inappropriate for work attire."

Mr. Tucker raises his eyebrows in surprise. He had noticed Ms. Cane when she arrived for duty, but he had not taken special note of her appearance. As the bus finishes unloading, he joins Mrs. Strain as she walks back toward the drop-off line. "I will see what the fuss is about and address it," Mr. Tucker assures Mrs. Strain.

When he arrives at the drop-off line, Mr. Tucker stands back to observe. Ms. Cane, a recent college graduate and one of his brand new teachers, is happily greeting arriving students and helping them move out of cars and toward the sidewalk. She smiles and waves at parents, and Mr. Tucker admits to himself that some of the parents have surprised—and disapproving—looks on their faces. Ms. Cane is wearing shoes with a heel—Mr. Tucker learns later from his assistant principal that these are called "wedge heels." She is also wearing a flowing see-through sundress that stops a little below mid-thigh. It has one strap that is about two inches wide. Mr. Tucker doesn't understand what the fuss is about. In his opinion, Ms. Cane looks nice and has dressed appropriately for her age. But, he has to admit that the looks on some of the faces of the parents disturb him. He decides that he will talk this over with his assistant principal, Mrs. Taylor, and then decide what to do.

As morning duty ends, Mr. Tucker finds himself busy with the myriad of small fires that need attention on the first day of school. Breakfast has run late because the younger students or new students are unfamiliar with procedures and don't know their student numbers. The first-grade classrooms have temporarily lost their Internet connection, so the teachers cannot take attendance or begin with any lessons that incorporate online resources. Three parents have arrived to enroll new students. The first time that Mr. Tucker is able to speak with Mrs. Taylor is during the lunch periods, while they are on duty supervising the students.

Mrs. Taylor listens intently as Mr. Tucker shares the events of the morning, and then she nods. "Yes, I have seen Ms. Cane today," Mrs. Taylor states, "and she does look very nice and appropriate for her age. However, she doesn't technically meet our dress code for teachers. Teachers are supposed to wear clothing that at least covers the top of the shoulders—we have said that they cannot wear 'sleeveless' shirts, and only those that span the shoulder and the only part that is missing is the sleeve."

Mr. Tucker nods and agrees that Ms. Cane's dress doesn't meet that requirement.

"But, that is not my biggest concern about Ms. Cane right now," continues Mrs. Taylor. "She seems to be having a rough morning with her students. Of course she is very nice and she is trying to build a rapport with them, but so far, I have observed several of her students running in the hallway while she was leading them to the library, and she did not redirect them; she did not take attendance until the front office clerk reminded her to do so; and one of her grade-level teammates had to go over to her classroom because it was so loud—and Ms. Cane was not in the room. She came back a couple of minutes later, saying that she had to step out to take a call on her cell phone!"

Mr. Tucker frowned. "I could excuse the failure to take attendance and maybe even the running in the hallway by chalking those things up to the fact that it's her first day. But, I am concerned that she left the students unsupervised to take a phone call."

Mrs. Taylor agreed. "We do need to address these issues quickly so that we can support her while also letting her know our expectations."

"I am not comfortable speaking with her about the dress code," Mr. Tucker expressed. "Do you mind having a conference with her this afternoon to speak with her about how her first day went and to address our concerns?"

"I will gladly do that," replied Mrs. Taylor. "I am also going to speak with Mrs. Beck. She is a veteran teacher in the grade level, and I think she would serve as a good mentor and role model for Ms. Cane."

"Excellent," affirmed Mr. Tucker. "I will wait to hear from you about how things go this afternoon."

That afternoon, Mrs. Taylor made her way to Ms. Cane's classroom.

By that time, the entire school was abuzz about what the new teacher was wearing.

"How was your first day?" Ms. Cane began.

"Well," Ms. Cane sighed, "It was overwhelming. I forgot all about taking attendance while I was trying to get to know the kids and take care of all of the first day paperwork. Then, I had more trouble with behavior than I was expecting on the first day. The kids were great, but it's like they were still in 'summer mode.' They were a little out of control by the end of the day! Plus, I guess I was a little distracted. I got a phone call that my grandfather had to go to the hospital, and it was hard to have that on my mind and still focus on the students."

"First of all," said Mrs. Taylor as she sat down in a chair. "How is your grandfather?"

"We think he is going to be okay," Ms. Cane shared as she also sat down. "He got a little dizzy, and they were afraid it was his heart. But they have run several tests and now they think he is just dehydrated."

"That's good news!" Mrs. Taylor exclaimed. "I do want you to know that if anything like that happens while you are teaching, all you have to do is let us know. Also, let your family know that they are always welcome to call the front office if they need you so that we can get you out of class immediately in an emergency—and we can send someone to supervise your students while you are dealing with whatever may arise."

Ms. Cane nodded sheepishly. "I know I shouldn't have left the students to step out and take the call, but I was afraid for my grandfather, and I thought everything would be okay. I am sorry that Ms. Lance had to come over to see what was going on."

Mrs. Taylor nodded. "This is a learning experience for you. No matter how 'good' the students seem, you should not leave students unsupervised. Your grade-level team is always happy to help out by keeping an eye on your students, and you can always call the office and we will send someone down.

"Now," Mrs. Taylor continued, "forgetting to take attendance on the first day is understandable. It could happen to the best of teachers. I do think you sound a little overwhelmed with the behavior and could use a little guidance with how to set up a good classroom management plan for your students."

"That would be nice," admitted Ms. Cane.

"It's something they really can't teach you in school. Learning to manage a classroom full of students is something that comes with experience. The good thing is we have some teachers who have been at this a long time, and they have learned some tricks of the trade. I am going to ask Mrs. Beck to work with you to help you develop a good plan for how to manage behavior in the classroom."

"I could use all the help I can get, I think," laughed Ms. Cane. "I just wasn't sure how to handle some of the more . . . 'active' kids today!"

"Mrs. Beck will be a good resource for you then," assured Mrs. Taylor. "Now, one more thing. When you got the faculty handbook, did you have time to review it all?"

"Well, to be honest," started Ms. Cane, "we got that on the same day that we learned how to set up our online gradebooks and how to set up our email. So, I spent a little time skimming it and I was going to come back to it. I haven't had a chance yet."

"I understand—taking in all of the information you get during preplanning is like trying to drink water from a firehose! I encourage you to go back to that handbook tonight and especially read the part about the dress code for teachers. There is nothing wrong with your outfit today—you look lovely. However, our dress code for teacher's states that tops cannot be sleeveless and must cover the top of the shoulders."

"Oh," Ms. Cane turned red. "I am so sorry! I never dreamed that this would not be appropriate!"

"I don't want you to be upset," Mrs. Taylor assured. "Again, you look lovely, and I understand that you just skimmed the dress code. Teaching is tough, and the first day is a trial by fire. But, you have a heart for kids, and the rest will fall into place."

Questions for Discussion

1. What issues arose on Ms. Cane's first day of teaching that needed to be addressed by an administrator? Which ones were more pressing or more urgent? Which might not have been so urgent?
2. Mr. Tucker asks Mrs. Taylor to be the one to address the dress code with Ms. Cane. Do you think this was appropriate? Discuss the pros and cons of having dress code matters addressed by administrators who are the same gender as the teacher.
3. What takes up most of Mr. Tucker's time on the first day of school? In reality, "small fires" can monopolize an administrator's time throughout the year. As an administrator, what strategies might you use to balance the "small fires" with the need to be an instructional supervisor?

4. Mrs. Taylor chooses to go to Ms. Cane's room for their afternoon "conference." Why would she do that? Explain how the environment—Ms. Cane's classroom versus Mrs. Taylor's office—would change the nature of the conversation.
5. What do you think about how Mrs. Taylor addressed the concerns that she and Mr. Tucker have with Ms. Cane? Would you have engaged in a similar conversation? What would you do differently? Critique Mrs. Taylor's leadership style based on this conversation.
6. One of the strategies that Mrs. Taylor uses to support Ms. Cane is assigning her a mentor—Mrs. Beck. What do you think of this approach? How do you think Ms. Cane will benefit from a mentor? What other strategies might you add to Mrs. Taylor's plan for Ms. Cane?
7. Does the faculty or staff dress code affect teaching and learning?
8. Is it important to have a professional dress code in schools? Why or why not?

Chapter Five

Technology Matters

CASE STUDY 5.1
YOUTUBE SHOW AND TELL

Standards 4.a and 4.b

Topic: Rural elementary school. This is a grade five social studies lesson on the Civil War. The issue here is Internet safety and protocol prior to having students work in online settings.

Mrs. Ryan was excited to see what Mr. Burston had come up with for his fifth-grade class. After years of battling cell phones in their elementary school, administrators at Northside Elementary finally decided to embrace technology. Most fifth graders at Northside already had iPads, so the school decided to make it mandatory for fifth graders and received a small grant to provide refurbished iPads to students who could not afford them. This was fairly easy to do considering the town Northside resided in was quite wealthy.

The idea was to integrate technology inside of the classroom and use the iPads daily in lessons and communication with both students and parents. Teachers received mandatory training at the beginning of the school year that coached them on at least twenty-five different apps that they could use inside the classroom, as well as how to encourage responsible technology use by the students. The apps out there were amazing; there was everything from safe teacher-student messaging to interactive whiteboards.

Northside Elementary was located in the small southern town of Caster outside of a major metropolitan city. The town was well educated; more than 93 percent had a college degree. The town itself was very quaint. It had historic, southern buildings and cute bed and breakfasts. It was often used as a background for filming of movies or television shows like *The Walking Dead*.

The school itself was fairly uniform, especially when considering socioeconomic status; only 5 percent of the school was on free and reduced lunch. The school was 60 percent Caucasian, 20 percent Asian, 5 percent Hispanic, and 15 percent other. Northside had a growing population of five hundred students; more and more people were moving to the town of Caster every year. People were attracted by the rural setting, affordable housing, and proximity to jobs in the major city. Besides, the schools, such as Northside, were some of the best in the state.

Northside was part of a relatively wealthy county, and the district was the highest rated in the state. Northside had a small special education and English language learner (ELL) population. In Mr. Burston's class, he had three special education students and two ELLs. This was about how many there were in each class in the school. There were two ELL teachers and three special education teachers for the whole building that split the caseloads to assist the general education teachers as needed.

Northside's decision to make iPads mandatory had been a controversial move on the school's behalf, especially given the school was elementary. However, the school had decided to roll out the expectation only with their fifth-graders. The idea was that rather than fighting with students about technology, they'd teach them how to use it appropriately.

This is why Mr. Burston's class was so exciting to watch today. Mr. Burston was a Millennial, and he'd fully embraced the idea of technology in the classroom. In fact, for the six years he'd taught at Northside, he had always been one of the "technology gurus" at the school. Although that wasn't his title, he was often the guy teachers turned to when they were having trouble with an iPad or laptop.

As Mrs. Ryan walked toward the classroom in Mr. Burston's room, she admired some of the class projects and posters adorning the walls. The school took special pride in keeping its projects updated around the school. With parents at home to help the students, the projects often turned out very nice. Outside of Mr. Burston's room, there were several tri-fold posters describing how to be a good citizen.

She walked inside of Mr. Burston's classroom, excited to see exactly how he was embracing the technology. This observation was important. Mrs. Ryan was to take some of the informal observations she was doing and present them to the Board of Education in a few weeks, especially given some of the controversy the iPads were causing.

When she walked inside of Mr. Burston's classroom, she was immediately pleased. There was a handwritten objective on the whiteboard at the front of the classroom, but the students were already integrating technology. All of the students were logged in on their iPads to the online classroom where Mr. Burston had uploaded an interactive lesson that had recorded his voice describing his lesson's objective. Mrs. Ryan immediately took out her cell phone so she could record a video of what was happening.

The voice on the iPads instructed the students to open up a different app in order to answer an opening question. Mrs. Ryan watched as the students swiftly changed to a new app. She looked over the shoulders of several students to see an opening question about the Civil War. There was both a multiple choice and short answer question. The students had five minutes to answer the questions and press "submit." A small timer ticked in the corners of the app as the students worked. While they typed, Mr. Burston sat at his desk with his own iPad. Mrs. Ryan strolled up to him to see what he was looking at. As the students virtually answered, he could see their answers on his screen. She walked back to the students working.

This time, however, she noticed several students had submitted their work and moved on to something else on their iPads. At least four students were playing games on their iPad while a few others were on social media or YouTube. Because the kids all had ear buds in order to listen to appropriate content, Mr. Burston didn't know whether students were on task or not.

Mrs. Ryan frowned; this was not good. After five minutes, Mr. Burston called the class to attention, and he began going over the answers to the opening question. The app that he had on his iPad, which he virtually displayed over a projector screen, showed all of the students' answers to the multiple choice question in a bar graph form (anonymously, of course). Most students had the right answer, as evidenced by the bar graph. Mr. Burston asked for a volunteer to explain why the answer was correct and then went over his two favorite short answers. Mr. Burston took about a minute to explain why he liked the short answers.

After going over the opening question, Mr. Burston asked the students to access the class workspace on their iPads. The class workspace was a spot where Mr. Burston frequently uploaded class documents for the class to peruse. This was an instruction the students were clearly used to doing because no one had a problem following this instruction. After about two minutes, the students all had a rubric pulled up on their iPads. Mr. Burston, who'd displayed the same rubric on the projector, went through the rubric. Mrs. Ryan noticed that most students followed Mr. Burston's instructions, but after they pulled up the rubrics, a few of the students around her switched back to video games or social media.

"Today, we are going to start a Civil War project," he said. "You will have the next five days to complete this project as a group in class. However, you may need to do some things at home. I will sort you into groups of three, and you will need to choose ten of these fifteen questions to answer about the Civil War." Mr. Burston walked to the projector screen and pointed out ten key questions. These questions included, "Explain the importance of the Gettysburg Address" and "What was the lasting impact on the South?"

"Today, you will get into your groups of three and choose the ten questions you want to answer and start researching the answers. You will log all of your answers on this worksheet," Mr. Burston said. With this, he passed out a worksheet that had all of the questions on it. Under each question, there were about five lines for an answer, as well as a spot for where the answer was found.

As Mr. Burston walked around to pass out the worksheets, Mrs. Ryan noticed that the student who had been playing his video game in front of her quickly switched to the rubric on his iPad. How Mr. Burston didn't notice, she wasn't sure. She was pretty sure he was too wrapped up in his own technology to really notice.

"Tomorrow we will start recording video with our iPads to answer these questions. You'll be able to answer these questions by choosing one of the following video formats: 1) a news broadcast, 2) a Civil War reenactment, or 3) a song or rap. If you have another amazing idea, please tell me, so I can approve," Mr. Burston said.

"To answer the questions today, you can search the Internet or use your textbook through your Kindle app. Wherever you get the answers from, you'll need to include that on the reference spot in your question sheet," Mr. Burston said. "I'll choose the two or three best videos from the class to introduce the topic to my class next year. Are there any questions?"

A few of the girls at the front of the room asked a few questions, mainly having to do with ideas about the video format. So far, Mrs. Ryan loved the creativity and use of technology. However, she had a few concerns about what was going on in the classroom. As Mr. Burston answered the students' questions, he did not walk around. Instead, he stayed rooted at the front of the room with his own iPad. Although he was using it to display his own iPad screen to answer the students' questions, it meant he was missing a lot of what was going around him. Many of the students were still goofing around on the iPads.

After answering the questions, Mr. Burston split the students into groups of three. Mrs. Ryan could tell that he had intentionally grouped the students, which is why he did not randomize it with an app he had on his iPad that could pick students at random. He had split the special education students and ELL students up so that they were well dispersed in the classroom. He'd placed at least one technology "guru" in each group.

"When I play music, I want you all to get into your groups," Mr. Burston instructed. "When the song is over, you should have your desks turned to each other with your iPads out."

When the music started, the students did as Mr. Burston asked. It grew, understandably, a bit louder in the classroom, but the students were in general pretty quiet and on task as they moved their desks and iPads into an appropriate formation. After the song ended, the class naturally quieted and looked to Mr. Burston for further instruction.

"You guys have the next thirty minutes to choose your ten questions and begin answering them," Mr. Burston said. "Today, I'd like you to finish at least seven of the questions, if not all of them. The more you do in class, the less you'll have to do at home. If you have any questions at all, please raise your hands, and I'll come to you. You have everything you need at your desks, so please don't get up. I also expect the voice level to stay at a conversation level. There is no reason to yell. Are there any questions about my expectations?"

There weren't, so Mr. Burston again played some soft acoustic tunes, and the students began working. At first, many of the kids were on task choosing their ten questions. However, as the students began researching, Mrs. Ryan noticed things began to go awry a bit. Mr. Burston was distracted at the front of the classroom with a student who was having an iPad issue. A group close to Mrs. Ryan started laughing and giggling to themselves. Mrs. Ryan craned her neck to see what they were giggling about. She could see a YouTube video playing on one of the student's iPads. On the YouTube video, there was a topless woman dancing.

The group snickered and pointed to the video. Mrs. Ryan decided it was time to intervene, so she walked over to the group of students and asked them to turn it off. She then confiscated the student's iPad who was displaying the video and told him to meet her in her office after class.

Mr. Burston, seeing the commotion, walked over to the group and asked Mrs. Ryan what was going on. She told him she'd tell him after class. The rest of the class went by without incident. Mr. Burston had fixed the iPad issue for the other student, but he stayed at his desk on his own iPad, apparently grading other assignments or working on class documents. Regardless, the class stayed relatively on task, and Mrs. Ryan noticed that almost all of the groups had at least seven of their questions answered by the end of the class period. After thirty minutes, Mr. Burston stopped the music, indicating work time was over.

He asked them all to write their names on their worksheets and walked around to collect them. "I'll hold onto these, so you don't lose them," he explained. "Tomorrow, we will finish answering the questions and begin shooting our videos. If you'll need any props, I do have some Civil War outfits." He swept a hand indicating a small closet in the room that had a few blue hats and coats. "However, if you need anything else, you'll need to bring it from home. For our closing activity, I want you to work with your groups to decide if anyone needs to bring anything from home. If you do, I want someone to message you through our class messaging system now to remind you what you need to bring."

Mrs. Ryan watched as the students deliberated among themselves. Then, a few of the students accessed the class message system to send reminders about what to bring. Class was then over, and they lined up a bit noisily to head to recess. Mrs. Ryan held the student back who'd been showing the inappropriate video. She called the parent, but she did give the iPad back. She assigned the student an after-school detention with her, and she left it at that. However, some things would need to change in Mr. Burston's class to prevent that from happening again.

The next day, Mrs. Ryan met with Mr. Burston to discuss the class she'd observed. She told him about the inappropriate video. Mr. Burston was stunned. He hadn't seen any of it happen. Mrs. Ryan explained that this was part of the issue she had with the lesson. Although she loved the use of technology, he was not supervising the students enough.

Mrs. Ryan suggested that Mr. Burston do a few things to implement improved technology use in his room. First of all, she suggested he walk around the classroom more. "You need to see what they are doing at all times. They may look on task, but a lot of times they aren't." Second of all, Mrs. Ryan suggested that Mr. Burston teach the students about Internet safety. She encouraged him to teach students about why they should avoid certain sites, even when they are in the privacy of their own homes. Mrs. Ryan also asked him to send an iPad Safety Agreement home to all students. She handed Mr. Burston a sample worksheet. Then, Mr. Burston asked her why there weren't better school-wide blocks on inappropriate sites, such as Facebook, Whisper, and Snapchat. Mrs. Ryan promised she would look into it.

Questions for Discussion

1. What do you think about mandating iPads for all students? What are the benefits? What are the risks?
2. What can the school do to support Mr. Burston and the other teachers with encouraging responsible technology use?
3. What else would you suggest to Mr. Burston to improve his lesson?
4. Would things did you like about the lesson?
5. How have you seen technology used in the classroom? When has it been a burden? When has it been a success?
6. Do you agree or disagree with how Mrs. Ryan punished the student who was watching the inappropriate YouTube video? Why or why not?
7. How could the incident with the student who was watching the inappropriate video have been prevented? What steps need to be taken so as to avoid this from happening in future lessons?

CASE STUDY 5.2
PHANTOM PHONES

Standards 4.c and 4.d

Topic: Suburban high school. This is about a grade ten Spanish 1 lesson on conjugating the verb ser. *This is about cyberbullying in the classroom and using preventive measures.*

Señora Fisher had received a double major in college: education and Spanish. She was quite passionate about the Spanish language, which is something she tried to instill in all of her students. While in college, she'd studied abroad in Spain for a year. She'd lived with a family in a small apartment in Madrid. It had been an experience that had changed her forever. Not only had she become passionate about the culture around her, she'd met her future husband. He'd eventually followed her back to the United States, but they made at least one pilgrimage a year back to Spain to visit his family with their two children.

This passion for the Spanish culture was something she tried desperately to bring into her classes, though it was not always an easy task. Señora Fisher had been teaching at Foster Heights High School for fourteen years. Prior to that, she'd taught at a failing urban school for three years. That had been a tough journey, but she'd learned all she knew from it. Señora Fisher was department head of the foreign language department at Foster Heights High School, and she also frequently held professional developments for other foreign language teachers in the districts. To put it bluntly, she was highly regarded in the district. Because of this, she was not at all concerned when Mr. Giovanni, the building's assistant principal, announced that he was coming to do his first semester observations. Señora Fisher's observations always went swimmingly.

However, Mr. Giovanni had a reputation that was beginning to circulate around the faculty. He had only been at Foster Heights High School for three months, but he was apparently a tough evaluator. Mr. Giovanni took his job seriously, and he had yet to give a "perfect" evaluation. Señora Fisher was convinced she could be the first.

As Señora Fisher prepared her classroom for her first period observation, she thought about how much happier she was at Foster than she'd been at her previous school so many years ago. Foster Heights High School was not a typical school. It was a magnet school for the district's advanced placement (AP) population. All students at Foster had an opportunity to take AP; 33 percent of the population at Foster was currently enrolled in an AP class. In fact, Señora Fisher taught three AP Spanish classes, as well as three Spanish 1 classes. Today, Mr. Giovanni was observing her teach Spanish 1.

Foster Heights was one of eight high schools in the large district located about thirty minutes outside of a large city in the southern United States. Almost 85 percent of its population was on free and reduced lunch, and 88 percent considered themselves a minority. The school was nationally recognized for its innovative program. The school was on a block schedule, with four seventy-minute periods each day. In addition, every other day students had a special "Bear Power Hour" time when they could work with a teacher in a subject they needed extra help with. Students were assigned to these classes based on what they considered their highest need.

Señora Fisher glanced at the clock to see that it was ten minutes to class. She heard the morning warning bell that signaled it was time for students to leave the cafeteria or gym for the classrooms. She knew Mr. Giovanni would be heading straight to her classroom after finishing his morning duty in the cafeteria.

She glanced around her room to make sure everything was set up appropriately. There were fifteen posters in the room (she'd counted at the beginning of the school year) that held a variety of Spanish content. That morning, she'd moved her poster about "*ser*," the lesson's subject of the day, to the front of the room. On the front white board, she'd drawn a line. On one side, she'd written the day's objectives for Spanish 1; on the other she'd written the objectives for AP Spanish. She also had a short agenda for each class. The desks, which were normally arranged to face the front of the room, were facing each other in groups. Each desk had a sticky note attached with a name of a student.

At the end of class, she'd instruct the students to take their names off the top, revealing the next student's name on the sticky note beneath. She switched the seating charts every quarter, and since this was the first day of the new quarter, she was due for a new seating chart anyway. Next to the whiteboard, she had her projector screen. On her laptop, at her desk, she had the YouTube video she planned to present. As students started to filter in, she repositioned herself to the door of the classroom in order to greet students as they came in.

"Hello, Juan! How was your weekend?" she said, giving all of the students' names a bit of Spanish flair if she could. As the students walked to their desks, she handed them each a thick packet. Señora Fisher thought of it as her "*Ser* packet," but the students had yet to discover this. She also gave them a handout that outlined the notes she would go through that day in class. As she stood at the door, the class settled in behind her.

She saw a few trying to inconspicuously finish their homework from the day before while others talked to their neighbors. Finally, the bell rang. She went to her desk to do attendance quickly. As she did this, she asked the students to study the objectives at the front of the room and discuss with their neighbor what they would be learning about. When Señora Fisher glanced up, Mr. Giovanni was walking into the room with a clipboard and his laptop in his arms.

As Mr. Giovanni settled himself into the back of the classroom, Señora Fisher introduced the topic in her usual bright manner: "*Hola clase* (Hello, class!)," she said. "Today we are going to learn about something new exciting! We are going to learn about our first verb: *ser*. Who's excited?"

"This morning, we are going to start with a video on *ser*. I want everyone to get out their Spanish notebooks to write some notes about *ser*." She flipped to her personal Spanish notebook that she used as an example for students and showed her page titled "*Ser* Video Notes" for some guidance. "Please remember to write where these notes are in your Table of Contents page at the front of your notebook. For me, they are on page thirty-one."

As the students did this, she turned on the projector and set up the video. Mr. Giovanni, who'd been scribbling away, noticed that during this dialogue she had remained at her desk. A few years ago, he knew Señora Fisher had suffered from a debilitating knee injury. Although she could walk, it often felt better to stay seated at her desk. Mr. Giovanni sighed as he settled in to watch the video. He knew his reputation at Foster was already growing as a "nitpicky" assistant principal. However, he believed that all students deserve the best education possible, and all teachers, no matter how experienced, had room to grow. He rarely, if ever, gave out perfect observations. This wasn't because he was nitpicky. It was because everyone could grow somehow.

Señora Fisher meanwhile asked one of her students to flip the lights to low so that the students would have enough light to write their notes. She watched from her desk as the students started scribbling in their notebooks. The video was about eight minutes long and contained several examples and charts that illustrated the use of *ser*. What Señora Fisher had liked about it was the video was set in Argentina and included several examples of Argentinian culture.

Mr. Giovanni decided he liked the video, but he noticed that a few of the students in the back were not writing notes. Instead, they had gotten their phones out and were scrolling through Facebook. Although he wasn't pleased with them, he decided to play ignorant and see if it became a learning experience for Señora Fisher. He noticed one student taking a photo for Snapchat.

After the video, Señora Fisher asked the students to get their homework out from the night before. As they got it out, Señora Fisher finally left her desk to check if each student had completed it. "I'm only checking for completion, not for accuracy," she said. "Please get out a different colored pen and grade yourselves now." When she arrived back to her desk, she put the homework page on the document camera with the correct answers. She sat back down and gave the students about three minutes to grade themselves.

After that, she asked the kids to get out their notes page that she'd handed them at the beginning of class. "I've already given you a completed notes page today, so I want you guys to just listen to the lecture," she said. "At the end of class, I'll pass out a stapler to staple these in your notebooks. Meanwhile, I want you to listen and add anything else in your notes."

With that, Señora Fisher switched her projector screen to a PowerPoint presentation about conjugating *ser*. The notes were already completed for the students, so there was not much for them to do but listen. Mr. Giovanni knew she did this for some of her special education students in the class but wondered if it provided the students with little incentive to listen. Because the students didn't have much direction with the notes, Mr. Giovanni noticed students scrolling through their phones again. This time, however, he saw at least six of the twenty-seven in the class on Facebook, Instagram, or Snapchat. Again, he didn't feel it was his place to reprimand the students in the class, but it was something he would bring up with Señora Fisher. In addition, he couldn't help but give one girl a stern look when she glanced at him; she did put the phone away after that.

Cell phones were not a new problem at Foster Heights, and they were a tough nut to crack. Parents wanted their kids to have them, especially in light of some of the school violence in recent years. However, more often than not, students were using them improperly or at the wrong time.

After the class notes, Señora Fisher asked the students to get out their "*Ser* packets" that she had provided at the beginning of class. The students were to work on their "*Ser* packets" with the three members of their group, which had already been assigned per Señora Fisher's sticky note seating chart. At this point, thirty-five minutes of the seventy-minute lesson had gone by. She gave the groups twenty minutes to complete two pages in the "*Ser* packet."

"I will not be available for questions," she said. "You must use your notes or your group members for support. You will turn this in so I can assess where the class is as a whole. During the group work, I do expect low voices. There should also not be any getting up for any reason. Does anyone have any questions before we begin?"

After she fielded a few questions, the students began to work. Señora Fisher, again, did not get up from her desk. After about fifteen minutes, several of the groups started to finish. They turned in their assignments to Señora Fisher, who immediately started to grade them, logging the answers into a spreadsheet to assess the class performance. However, the students who were finished had no further instructions. A few students were whispering quietly to each other, while the others sat again on their cell phones.

After the twenty minutes, Señora Fisher gathered the remaining worksheets from the students and asked them to put on their "listening ears." Mr. Giovanni noticed the students with cell phones out put them away to listen.

She then read a brief dialogue between two people. Señora Fisher read the dialogue aloud and asked students to raise their hands when they heard a conjugated verb. Next, she read aloud the dialogue again, but this time, she asked students to write down everything they heard. "I'll grade it for completion," she clarified to the class as they looked around nervously.

She then reread the dialogue two or three more times so all of the students could get it. After the students completed the activity and turned it in, Señora Fisher polished off the class with just as bright of a closure as she'd opened it with: "I'm so proud of you all for learning how to do this so quickly! *Ser* is not easy, so you guys are doing great!" Thirty seconds later, the bell rang, and the class was dismissed. As Mr. Giovanni left the classroom, he arranged with Señora Fisher to meet with her the following day after school.

Two hours after Mr. Giovanni arrived back from Señora Fisher's observation, a distraught tenth-grader came into his office, crying her eyes out. "Mr. Giovanni," she sobbed. "Savannah was on Facebook this morning calling me a slut." Mr. Giovanni asked to see the Facebook post on Savannah's phone and took a picture for documentation. Sure enough, the post was there on Savannah's wall, and the time stamp was 8:52 a.m., when Savannah was sitting in Señora Fisher's classroom. Mr. Giovanni's day was filled with the melodrama of this affair, but he knew that what he had to talk to Señora Fisher about was even more serious.

The next day, Señora Fisher arrived in Mr. Giovanni's office right on time. However, he was running a bit late due to the drama with the Facebook post. When Señora Fisher settled in, Mr. Giovanni began: "Señora Fisher, your lesson had a lot of strong points. I thought you had a good mix of cultural elements, verb conjugation, and listening exercises. However, we have a major problem." Mr. Giovanni went on to discuss the seriousness of the Facebook post that was posted in her room on her watch.

Mr. Giovanni told Señora Fisher that he believed she needed to do several things to improve the overall engagement in her class. Señora Fisher, who had been so confident in her lesson, was distraught. She'd never had such a negative observation, but she saw the truth in Mr. Giovanni's words. Señora Fisher promised to improve the situation with his suggestions.

Questions for Discussion

1. What suggestions for improvement should Mr. Giovanni give to Señora Fisher?
2. Would you have interfered with the Facebook posters if you'd been Mr. Giovanni? Why or why not?
3. Because Mr. Giovanni did not interfere, is it fair to blame Señora Fisher completely for the cyberbullying situation?

4. What do you think of Mr. Giovanni's suggestions? Would you have any suggestions to add?
5. Have you dealt with any cyberbullying issues before in the school? If so, how did you manage the problem?
6. What did you like about Señora Fisher's lesson? What did you dislike? Why?

CASE STUDY 5.3
QUESTIONS AND ANSWERS

Standards 2.f and 4.d

Topic: Rural middle school. This is about a grade eight science lesson on materials science and the proper utilization of film in a classroom.

Mr. Baker was considered a bit of a mad scientist among his pupils. He had been teaching in the same school for seven years, and his lessons were well known for being energetic and fun—and easy. Students always learned something in Mr. Baker's lesson, and they did well in their exams, many even went on to study chemistry successfully in high school, having a good set of basic skills. They were just never really required to think independently that often, and perhaps it was this very reason that his middle school pupils, their minds already preoccupied with dances, dating, and fitting in, found his classes enjoyable. They were entertained by Mr. Baker's crazy ties, his mismatched socks, the way he was always misplacing his glasses, and the fact that he often had a pencil behind each ear and sometimes one even stuck through his beard!

"Good morning, grade eight." Mr. Baker greeted his class, his tie a little crooked and sporting a small coffee stain already, his glasses shoved on the top of his head making his sandy colored hair stick out at funny angles.

"Good morning, Mr. Baker," they replied in unison.

"Take a seat. Leave your books closed; you won't need them straight away."

The class obeyed and settled into their seats as Mr. Baker turned on the projector at the front of the room to reveal a film with the "play" icon waiting to be pressed.

"Yessss!" came the response from the class, they loved watching films in Mr. Baker's class; he actually chose ones that students liked. They were funny and entertaining, disguising the fact they were supposed to be learning something.

"Don't get too excited," Mr. Baker responded. "It's only a short one today. Just twenty minutes. And there is a worksheet for you to complete while watching."

He handed small piles of worksheets to various students.

"Take one and pass the pile on," he instructed, and the students did as they were told. They glanced at the title on the worksheet, "Solids, Liquids, and Gases," and Mr. Baker pressed play and flicked off the lights.

The short film lived up to expectations, it was a funny cartoon explaining the differences between the materials, and a funny cartoon about gases couldn't be done without offering up some old-fashioned toilet humor. Mr. Baker laughed along with his pupils, but he didn't seem to notice that nobody was answering the questions on the worksheet.

Twenty minutes later, the film ended and the lights came back on.

"Right," Mr. Baker began. "Question one. Name one property of a solid."

The class sat in silence. If Mr. Baker was to move from his post at the front of the room, he would have realized that not one student had filled in the worksheet. Some students were on their phones, but he could not see that. He asked the question again.

"Anyone got an answer? A property of a solid?"

Still nothing. Not wanting to waste time, Mr. Baker moved on.

"It has a set, defined shape." He answered his own question, and his students frantically copied the answer down.

"Moving on to question two. A property of a liquid?" Again silence filled the room, and it wasn't long before Mr. Baker found it unbearable.

"A liquid will take the shape of its container," Mr. Baker offered. The students wrote the answer down.

The rest of the lesson continued very much like this, and by the end of the period all twenty-eight students had exactly the same answers written on their sheets. They had texted each other the answers.

"Please glue your worksheets in and leave your books on the table by the door on your way out." Mr. Baker gave the orders just as the bell rang, and his class hurried to complete the task and get to their next lesson on time.

That afternoon, Mr. Baker sat down with a piece of banana cake and a fresh cup of coffee to look through his grade eight books. He marked their books regularly to ensure they understood the topic. He had only marked a few and was initially very impressed at how accurate the answers were, but he soon realized that every student had used his answers. He thought back to second period. He had shown the film, then gone through the worksheet, and yes, he now recalled the awkward silence that followed each time he asked a question. *Oh well*, he thought to himself, *at least they will have the information correct when it comes time to review for their exams.*

The next science lesson came around, and Mr. Baker's students entered the room and were shocked. The boring rows of desks that they sat in according to their seating plan had been transformed into groups, and on each group of desks was colored butcher paper, colored pens, scissors, and glue. The class didn't know where to go, so they just stood and waited for instructions from Mr. Baker.

"Don't just stand there looking like fools," his friendly voice boomed from the front of the room, his red pen sticking out from his beard. "Take a seat." His students looked at each other and shrugged. They did as they were told and chose seats next to their friends. Mr. Baker began his lesson.

"Each table will be allocated a material. There are six groups, so two groups will be doing the same material." He walked around and allocated each group a solid, liquid, or gas.

"Using what you learned yesterday, work together to create an informative poster on the colored butcher paper. You can use smaller pieces to decorate it, and you must include written information and pictures." Mr. Baker gave clear directions, and the groups began discussing. He was impressed to see his students so eager and left them to it for a while.

"I don't remember much from yesterday," Jess spoke to her group. "I just waited for Mr. Baker to give the correct answer and then I wrote it down. I didn't think a lot."

"I did the same," Jude replied.

"Me too," added Simone, "and Mr. Baker still has our books."

The group set about writing a large heading, using lots of colors, and began chatting.

"Have you done your history homework?" Simone asked Jess.

"Yeah, it took me ages though," she replied. "You?"

"Yep."

"Can I borrow your book at lunch then Simone?" Jude asked. "I didn't get a chance to finish."

"Sure," Simone replied.

The same type of conversations was taking place at each group. The fact that no one had to think for themselves yesterday meant that they had not stored a whole lot of information. Mr. Baker looked up from his desk at the front of the room and saw his pupils working away. A few minutes later he got up and went to check out what wonderful masterpieces his class had created. Most had only done a heading and a few sub-headings. They were wonderful though: artistic writing, full of color, and some groups had even cut the letters out of the smaller pieces of colored paper.

The only problem was that they lacked any actual information. Mr. Baker went from group to group offering up information and answers. In some cases, he even wrote notes on a piece of paper, leaving it for the students to copy. By the end of the lesson, Mr. Baker was in possession of six large posters, two each on solids, liquids, and gases. He was pleased with the results; it had been a little more than planned on his part, but he could put the posters up on the display board safe in the knowledge that the information was correct.

"Well that wasn't too hard," Jess said to Simone as they walked out the door.

"Yeah, Mr. Baker practically did it all; we just made it pretty!"

The girls giggled as they walked to their next lesson.

Mr. Baker was flicking through his resource folder trying to find an appropriate experiment to do with his grade eight class. They were bright but seemed to be struggling to retain information. He had heard that some of his colleagues were allowing their students to come up with their own experiments, so he decided the idea was worth trying.

The next science lesson, the students were a little disappointed to see the classroom arranged back in rows. They took their allocated seats and stared at the projector at the front of the room.

"Take out your practical books, please," Mr. Baker instructed.

"Yay!" The class cheered enthusiastically, it had been ages since they had done an experiment. Mr. Baker turned on the projector and a hush came over the class. There was no experiment written, only headings. A confused look appeared on their faces. Mr. Baker addressed them.

"You are to use the headings as a reminder and write your own experiment to investigate more about solids, liquids, and gases."

The class let out a collective groan.

"You will then carry out your experiments next lesson," Mr. Baker concluded, and that seemed to appease them. The students got to work.

"What's a hypothesis?" Jude whispered to Evan.

"No clue," he replied. "I can't remember anything. I know what equipment is, but I can't remember the proper names of stuff."

"How are we supposed to write results?" Jess asked Tori.

"I think you guess them now, and then change it later if it's wrong."

"That doesn't sound right," Jess queried.

"I'm just guessing that; I don't actually know. I can't remember."

The class either bumbled their way through the work, taking guesses, or left the page blank, waiting for Mr. Baker to offer up some more information. Simone was the first to raise her hand.

"Mr. Baker," she asked. "Can you please remind me what you have to write for the aim?"

"Sure," he replied. "It's what you hope to find out from the experiment. For example, what happens to liquid when you pour it into different shaped containers."

The whole class quickly scribbled down the example.

"And what's a hypothesis again?" Jude asked. He wasn't embarrassed any more, because asking the question worked for Simone.

"It's what you think will happen; it doesn't matter if you're wrong. If you were to write a hypothesis on the example I gave earlier you would write something like, 'I think the liquid will be the same shape as the container I pour it into,'" he offered. Once again, the class wrote the answer in their practical books.

Without even realizing it, Mr. Baker had soon created an experiment for his class. The students were excited that they would be doing a practical experiment next lesson, and they didn't even have to think!

The day of the experiment came, and Mr. Baker had written the list of equipment the students would be using on the board as a reminder. He asked them to set up their lab tables with all the necessary equipment, but his students struggled and stood around feeling useless.

"I don't know what a conical flask looks like," Evan whispered to Jude.

"Just wait a bit," Jude replied. "I'm sure Mr. Baker will tell us in a minute."

Sure enough, Mr. Baker couldn't handle the confused look of his pupils for long, and not wanting to waste valuable experiment time, he got out the equipment on his lab table at the front.

"Told ya," whispered Jude.

Mr. Baker patiently led his class through the experiment, carefully demonstrating each step at the front of the room. His students followed along meticulously; they were hard workers and keen to impress but it didn't stop them getting a little bored.

"I wish we could do more of our own stuff," Jess said to Simone as they were packing up.

"I agree," Simone replied. "Mr. Mackenzie's class gets to do way cooler experiments."

"I know."

The class tidied away their lab desks and sat back at their tables ready to record their homework in their planners. Mr. Baker wrote on the board.

Grade eight homework:
Complete experiment by writing the results and conclusion.
Draw a labeled diagram of the experiment.
Review for quiz on solids, liquids, and gases.

Questions for Discussion

1. Was Mr. Baker actually helping his pupils by offering them the answers all the time?
2. How could Mr. Baker get over his fear of silence in the classroom?
3. What could Mr. Baker have done to make the group work poster project a little easier for his students, rather than giving them the answers?
4. Could Mr. Baker's approach lead to any danger in the science laboratory when doing experiments?

5. Do you think many of Mr. Baker's students will be able to successfully complete their homework?
6. What could the teacher do about the students texting each other the answers?

CASE STUDY 5.4
THE ANSWER IS IN THE PHONE

Standards 2.b, 3.d, 4.e, and 4.f

Topic: Urban high school. This is a lesson about grade eleven students taking a science exam on the rock cycle and the issues that arise when students are cheating using technology.

Mr. Dell had been an assistant principal at the Peabody School for Excellence for six years. Peabody was an innovative school in the midst of a very large urban school district in the Midwest. Holster Public Schools, Peabody's district, was full of scandal. Recently, the district had been in the news for a huge corruption case involving over $2 million. Teachers were often striking or walking out, and there was always a new plan to unroll in order to better the district. Overall, the district ranked the lowest performing in the state, and no matter what the district did, things didn't seem to improve. Mr. Dell tried to stay out of all of these affairs. His priority was the students, and it always had been.

Mr. Dell, like most of the students at Peabody, was African American and raised in the city of Holster. He'd grown up in a family of six; he was the last born of four boys. His father had worked hard in a local auto plant welding together parts, and his mother had been a seamstress at a garment factory. However, now many of those plants had since closed, which had left the city in distress.

Peabody was unique, however. Despite the district's overall problems, Peabody managed to stay on top of things. In the late 1990s, Peabody had restructured and modeled itself after a collegiate school. To get into the school, students had to pass a district-wide examination. While at Peabody, they were required to maintain a 2.5 grade point average.

The students who graduated from Peabody were all accepted into colleges, many on scholarships. The school was not very diverse; over 98 percent of the students were African American. There were only a small handful of special education students. Compared to the rest of the district, the school had a fairly affluent population; only 35 percent of the students were on free and reduced lunch. Its graduation and attendance numbers were well over the national average at 98 percent. However, despite all of these things in their favor, the students still struggled to meet requirements on state testing, especially in science. On the previous year's exam, 78 percent of the students did not pass the state's requirements on the science portion of the exam. The administrators at Peabody had recognized this immediately and decided to put a lot of focus on its science program this year.

Today, an icy day in February, Mr. Dell had decided to visit Mrs. O'Keefe's classroom. Mrs. O'Keefe taught Earth sciences. She'd been at Peabody only a year, but she'd been teaching for over five. She'd relocated from another school in the district that had even more issues than Peabody. She'd been an integral part of the science restructuring program at Peabody. Mr. Dell had been in Mrs. O'Keefe's classroom dozens of times and thought she was truly an astounding science teacher.

Mrs. O'Keefe was the type of science teacher who tried to get her students engaged with every subject matter she taught. She was organized and meticulous with her methods. Her lesson plans were on time and on target. Because of this, the school was considering making her department head the next year and work a little less in the classroom. This was partially the purpose of Mr. Dell's visit today. He wanted to ensure that Mrs. O'Keefe was ready for such a challenge. The observation was a surprise; Mrs. O'Keefe was not expecting him. Although she had submitted her lesson plans to him on Monday, he had not had a chance to check what was on her agenda for that day.

As Mr. Dell walked down the hall toward Mrs. O'Keefe's second period class, he admired the school he was such an integral part of. The strict performance standards and insurance policy that students would go to college after graduating from Peabody meant that most of the students were fairly obedient. Although Mr. Dell was walking down the hall during a class change, the mass chaos that usually occurred during this transition at most schools wasn't a problem at Peabody. There was talking and gossip, of course, but students weren't overly loud; no one was in their lockers blocking the use of the halls.

Everyone was walking on the right side of the hallway, and all of the students were in their uniforms of khaki pants and a navy Peabody polo. Around the hall, there were bright posters that advertised school dances and fund-raisers. All were fairly well-made and eye-catching. There were a few motivational posters and loads of class work. Mr. Dell stopped to admire the wall outside one of the art classrooms. Peabody actually had an award-winning art program; many of the students who graduated went on to a local art institute. It was an amazing, rewarding place to work.

When Mr. Dell reached Mrs. O'Keefe's door, he noticed she was standing at the doorway greeting students and monitoring the hallway. He greeted her as he walked in and made his way to the back of the classroom. He noticed a "Do Now" on the board along with a class objective. Today, the class was going to take a unit exam on the rock cycle. Mr. Dell inwardly groaned; he hated monitoring tests. "Oh well," he thought. "Too late to turn back now."

Mr. Dell noticed that the "Do Now" on the board asked students to study their notes in preparation for the exam. All of the kids were doing just that: flash cards were being flipped, notebooks scanned through, and occasional scribbling. You could hear a pin drop in the classroom; except for the hallway noise, it was very quiet. The students were obviously focused.

Eventually, the bell rang, and Mrs. O'Keefe walked in. She silently went to her computer to do attendance and then glanced up. "I'll give you all five more minutes," she said quietly. She set a large timer on her computer that projected to the front of the room. The students continued their frantic studying, and Mrs. O'Keefe sat at her desk grading papers. When the timer went off, a few of the students groaned.

"Okay, class, it is time," Mrs. O'Keefe said. "I need all desks clear. Please remove all papers, textbooks, and notebooks. All I should see is a pencil. I need all materials put under your desk with no notes visible."

The students complied.

"Before we begin, I will allow two questions. Does anyone have a burning question about the material that they need answered? Turn to your neighbor and find out."

This was clearly something Mrs. O'Keefe did regularly because at that, all of the students turned to each other and started talking. After about a minute, the students seemed to have come to a consensus. One girl with braids at the front of the room raised her hand, "Mrs. O'Keefe, we just have one question: we'd like you to clarify the difference between igneous and metamorphic rocks."

Mrs. O'Keefe spoke for about two minutes about the difference and even included a very simple diagram on the board at the front of the room. After her explanation, she said, "I hope that will help you on this exam. Now, I am going to pass this out. You will have the remainder of class, sixty minutes, to finish the exam.

"There will be no time extension allowed. There are twenty multiple choice, two short answer, and one open response question. There should be no talking while the exam is on your table. If you finish early, please turn it into me and grab a textbook. You should begin reading pages forty to fifty-five, which you'll complete for homework." Mrs. O'Keefe gestured toward a towering stack of science textbooks on her desk. She began passing out the exam, and the class immediately was filled with the sounds of scribbling.

Mr. Dell tried to sit observing as quietly as possible. Normally, he liked to walk around, but he was afraid of distracting the students while they tested. He decided to move locations very slowly. As he sat and watched, he noticed that the students were using some of the multiple choice tactics many of the teachers regularly went over with them: process of elimination or underlining key words. The students were clearly taking the exam seriously, as they all seemed to take their time with the test.

After passing out the tests, Mrs. O'Keefe was back at her desk. She seemed to, again, be grading papers. Mr. Dell decided to change locations very slowly in order to better monitor the students. He got up slowly and walked toward the right side of the room. Just as he was passing Demarcus, he noticed him putting something swiftly in his pocket, and he saw Sheila's hand in her pocket. He couldn't be sure, but he thought they might be texting. He continued his post for five more minutes, but nothing else unusual seemed to occur. Mr. Dell walked slowly to the left side of the room but kept his eyes on Demarcus and Sheila. This time, he noticed Antwan's hand also in his pocket, though his eyes stayed trained on the paper. He was texting without looking at his phone! Mr. Dell pretended to turn away for a minute, and as he snuck a glance, he noticed Demarcus stealing a glance at his phone and then scribbling again.

Mr. Dell knew the students were cheating with their phones, but he did not want to disrupt the other students testing by making a big deal about it during the test. Instead, he decided to pass a note to Mrs. O'Keefe telling her of the situation. When he handed her the note, she nodded slightly.

Mr. Dell continued to walk around the classroom, but he didn't notice anyone else involved in the scandal. After about thirty minutes, students began to finish the test. They brought the exams to Mrs. O'Keefe who handed them a textbook and pointed at the directed reading listed on the board. Antwan, Demarcus, and Sheila continued working until the forty-five-minute mark, after which they all seemed to finish the exam within three minutes of each other. When they turned in their tests, Mr. Dell noticed that Mrs. O'Keefe whispered something to them. Mr. Dell assumed that it was to see her after class. They sat nervously at their desks attempting to read, but Mr. Dell noticed that there were no more hands in their pockets, and they all three seemed distracted.

When the bell rang, those three remained at their desks. Luckily, Mrs. O'Keefe had a planning period after their class, so she and Mr. Dell had a private spot to confront the three students. Once they had closed the door, Mr. Dell immediately asked to see all three of their phones. He switched to the messages and saw the evidence in Antwan's phone. There it had a few texts discussing the answers to several multiple choice questions. Demarcus's phone showed the same three-way conversation. There was no evidence in Sheila's phone; she had likely deleted the text. However, her name was clearly part of the conversations in both Antwan's and Demarcus's phones.

When asked, the students explained they felt a lot of pressure to maintain their grade point average. In particular, Antwan said his parents were getting a divorce, so his grades had recently been slipping. He was trying to maintain a good grade point average in order to get a scholarship for his phenomenal artistic skills. All three were almost in tears. Mr. Dell felt for them, but the behavior was unacceptable. He told the three students to wait there for a minute while he conferenced with Mrs. O'Keefe about an appropriate punishment out in the hallway.

In the hallway, Mrs. O'Keefe and Mr. Dell decided to punish the students in four ways: all three would receive a zero on the test, the parents of all three would be notified with the recommendation that cell phones be confiscated for a week or two by the parents, each would have to serve one week of after-school detentions (missing any after-school activities), and all three would be put on probation. Another infraction would put the kids out of school. Although the students were ultimately to blame for the behavior, Mr. Dell couldn't help but feel like both the school and the teacher hadn't done enough to prevent such infractions from taking place.

Mrs. O'Keefe should have been walking around; it was clear she didn't make a habit of walking around. If she had, the students would have never attempted the scandal in the first place. Mr. Dell also couldn't help but wonder if the school was doing enough to dissuade students from doing such shenanigans. He wondered if the school should have a stricter phone policy during tests or a better, more clear punishment in case students were caught.

Questions for Discussion

1. How has the age of technology changed cheating in the classroom?
2. Do you feel the punishment was appropriate for the students? Why or why not?
3. What more could the school do to dissuade students from cheating?
4. What more could Mrs. O'Keefe do to prevent students from cheating in her classroom?
5. Given Mrs. O'Keefe's mistakes, would you promote her to department head? Why or why not?
6. Have you ever caught students in a cheating scandal? How did you address the infractions?

CASE STUDY 5.5
FACEBOOK TRAUMA

Standard 4.e

Topic: Urban high school. This is a case about a grade nine classroom studying personal finance in social studies. This is about students posting to Facebook during class time.

Mrs. Kelly was excited for today's lesson. She has been teaching for almost twenty years, and the use of the computer room has often eluded her. It's not that she doesn't like computers; she uses one rather frequently to type her lesson plans, add student information on to the school database, show relevant YouTube videos, write her reports, and send and receive emails, and she browses the Internet often enough. It's more that she is afraid of coming across as unintelligent to her pupils. She knows that teenagers these days know far more about how these sorts of things work, and she has become accustomed to being treated with the respect that a teacher in a long-standing position like hers has worked hard to achieve.

Mrs. Kelly has a reputation for being unforgiving on missed deadlines, for not allowing interruptions to her lessons, and certainly not tolerating tardiness. She believes that her tough teaching approach early on has made for slightly easier work when it comes to behavior management this far down the line. Despite her toughness, many of her pupils like her. They know where they stand as her guidelines are clear and unchanging. She doesn't have favorites, taking the same hard line with all rule breakers. Today, while maintaining her extreme air of professionalism, Mrs. Kelly was trying something new.

Shiloh Huron, another teacher and Mrs. Kelly's niece, created a lesson for her grade nine pupils to teach them about personal finance. Her inner-city school decided that more needed to be done to help drive the students away from the poverty line that so many of them had been born into. Shiloh had spent quite a while putting together the lead-up PowerPoint presentation along with the booklet for the students to complete. She had spent time on the Internet looking at appropriate resources and was pleased to report that her lessons had been a success.

"It was so nice to see the students engaged in something that was actually relevant to them," she told her aunt. "They didn't question the reason of the activity once!"

"How many lessons did you need to complete the activity?" Mrs. Kelly enquired, the cogs in her brain already turning with the idea that she could try Shiloh's idea.

"It took three all together," Shiloh replied, pleased that her role model teacher aunt was taking such an interest. "One to deliver the initial presentation and idea, then two to complete the task in the computer room."

"It sounds great," Mrs. Kelly said with a grin, "and you could assess their work easy enough?"

"Oh sure," Shiloh was beaming at this point. "I had them print it out and hand me a hard copy so I could take it home to mark. The only problem was that as part of the task must be completed at home, some pupils haven't handed me anything. I'm hoping they might catch up over the Christmas break."

Mrs. Kelly pondered this idea for a while. She had never taken a class to the computer room, and she was excited about using the lesson.

Mrs. Kelly had looked through the presentation and the booklet, and it all seemed rather straightforward. The students first learned about needs versus wants and were given examples of each as well as the suggestion that this is how they should prioritize their money when creating their own budgets. Then came the fun part. The students were to go home and measure their bedroom, including any built-in furniture. They would then return to school and use the computers in the computer room to redesign their bedroom.

They would be given a hypothetical seven hundred dollars to "buy" furniture and accessories. The two major guidelines were that the furniture had to fit the dimensions of their existing space (they would provide a drawing of the room layout in their booklet) and that they had to include the stipulated list of needs. Mrs. Kelly was keen to try the lessons, even though she wasn't exactly sure how the students would manage to find furniture and accessories via the Internet, but she had heard of people "online shopping" and knew that her group of fourteen- and fifteen-year-olds were much more savvy than she.

Mrs. Kelly had asked a fellow colleague to show her how to use the online school database to reserve a computer room for her lessons, and she delivered the PowerPoint presentation with all the confidence of a teacher of her experience and reputation.

She arrived at the computer room early to ensure she could get into the room without embarrassment of forgetting the code for the keypad in front of the class. She checked that all the computers had the little blue light on to indicate that they were working and stood in bewilderment at all the cords and the fancy sound and projection systems. The bell for third period rang and in moments her ninth-grade class was milling about outside comparing dimensions of their bedrooms.

The lesson started well; all but two of her students had completed the homework part of the task. She issued her usual detention, but decided to create dimensions for them in order to allow them to carry on with part two of the activity and not cause further delay. It was also decided that these pupils would lose 10 percent of their grade for their lack of homework. The students set about logging into their accounts on their computers with no problems, which came as a great relief to Mrs. Kelly as this meant she did not have to admit her lack of computer knowledge to her students. Everyone had their work booklets in front of them and had set about tapping hurriedly on the keyboard and clicking the mouse with vigor. Impressed with her students' enthusiasm, Mrs. Kelly did a lap around the computer room and saw a range of websites selling bedroom furniture: Walmart, Macy's, Target, Bed, Bath and Beyond, and IKEA, just to name a few.

Mrs. Kelly noticed that some students were spending as little as possible on their list of "needs," buying from the cheap, lower-quality retailers with the vision to spend the majority of their budgets on wants such as televisions, fancy mirrors, disco lights, and other ridiculous yet wonderful accessories that most teenagers would purchase if they were given half the chance. She was looking forward to seeing their final results and couldn't help but wonder if it would give her an insight to her pupils' priorities and personalities. Feeling relieved that things were under control and her students were working diligently, she returned to the main computer at the front of the room.

Mrs. Kelly logged into the computer and slipped into a comfort zone that she had not experienced before. She glanced up and could see all her students clicking and tapping away and could not resist the temptation to get a bit of work done herself. She checked her inbox and found two emails requiring fairly urgent attention. The first from her department head notifying her team of the agenda for the upcoming department meeting. She had some matters that had recently arisen that she was desperate to discuss and was thankful for the opportunity to respond to the email promptly and have a greater chance of her points being added to the agenda. The second was from an ex-student who was asking her to write a reference for a university application. Mrs. Kelly was flattered that so many of her old students still thought highly enough of her to ask her to do such things.

She set about responding to the emails, glancing at the class every now and again, always impressed at how involved in their work they were. However, because Mrs. Kelly was not actively walking around the class room, she did not notice several things. Her students, even though they were well-meaning and respectful teenagers, took the opportunity of the lack of supervision from their esteemed teacher and happily browsed the Internet freely. Many students had the smarts to keep one relevant tab open at the bottom of the screen, ready to click on it should Mrs. Kelly arise from the computer at the front and decide to make the rounds.

Tayla and Maddy were using the opportunity to catch up on a history assignment that was due, Ethan and Logan were on YouTube sniggering quietly at videos played on silent, and Stella, Jasmine, and Molly were browsing the latest hairstyles on Pinterest. This was perhaps all very harmless, other than the fact they weren't completing their work for Mrs. Kelly. However, in one corner of the room, Ethan had discovered the password to Jocelyn's Facebook page and had set about writing several false posts of rather a vulgar nature.

Before Mrs. Kelly knew it, the bell sounded to signal the end of the lesson and she had accomplished a good amount of work herself. The class packed away quickly, and she dismissed them with the reminder to meet at the computer room next lesson in order to complete their task. She did one lap around the room to check that no one had left any valuable belongings behind and that all the computers had been logged out correctly. Satisfied that the room was being left as she found it, she left, checking and double-checking that the door was locked behind her.

Mrs. Kelly spent the rest of the school day in a bit of a daze. She was able to manage her afternoon classes without any problems, her years of experience and tried and tested lessons working to her advantage. However, she had a constant strange feeling that she was forgetting something. She read through her "to do" list several times, but nothing was amiss there. It wasn't until the school day had ended and she sat down to check her emails that she recalled that she had already replied to a few crucial ones. Never before had she been able to respond so rapidly to emails that it had sent her off kilter for the rest of the day. She got to work replying to the last few emails that required her attention, checked she had everything in order for tomorrow, and headed home where she phoned Shiloh to give an update on how her computer room lesson had gone.

The next morning upon her arrival to school, she received a phone call from the principal asking her to stop by and see him immediately. Mrs. Kelly felt like one of her naughty students, wracking her brain as to why Mr. Hyslop would want to meet with her. She knocked confidently on his door, assuring herself that it must be some trivial matter that just needed discussing sooner rather than later. Mr. Hyslop opened the door and asked her to come in and take a seat. He joined her at the meeting table in the corner of his office and produced a few printed sheets of paper.

The first was a printout of a Facebook page. Mrs. Kelly was not a Facebook user, but she could recognize the layout as her own children were often on Facebook as well as her husband. Mr. Hyslop asked her to read the posts on the page, and she did so without hesitation. She was mortified. Jocelyn Henderson was a sweet girl, and the language used to describe what she liked to do to herself was beyond belief.

"This is awful, this is not the Jocelyn I know," she commented to Mr. Hyslop.

"I agree. However, I know for a fact that Jocelyn did not write these posts. Here read this."

He slid another piece of paper across the desk. It was an email from Jocelyn's mother. It went on to describe poor Jocelyn's shock and despair when she checked her Facebook account. She had thrown her iPhone across the room and retreated to her bedroom where she spent the entire night. Jocelyn's mother had read the offending posts on her daughter's phone and tried to plead with her to come out of her room to talk about it, but to no avail. Jocelyn only screamed through the door that she was never going to leave her room. Mrs. Henderson had included several screenshots of the posts, placing blame on the school as it can clearly be seen that the posts had been made during school hours; she believes the school should do some investigative work. Mrs. Kelly was, naturally, saddened by this but was trying to work out what all of this had to do with her meeting Mr. Hyslop at seven o'clock in the morning. Mr. Hyslop went on.

"We investigated further into the situation last night. Our first assumption was that maybe Jocelyn's phone had fallen into the wrong hands, but we thought we'd best check the use of the school computers." He paused as he flicked through a few pages. "One of the information technology guys went through all the computer log-ins for the time of day the posts were written and narrowed it down. He was able to see which websites students were accessing in this given time frame. Our computer room records show you had your social studies lesson yesterday in computer room B. Is this correct?"

"Yes," Mrs. Kelly replied. "They were given a task on the topic of personal finance."

"How many students completed the task satisfactorily?"

"I'm not sure yet. There are several parts to the task, and they have one more computer lesson to go."

"I'm afraid almost half your class was accessing sites deemed irrelevant to their subject content," Mr. Hyslop went on, handing her more documents that highlighted the sites that each individual computer had been using.

Questions for Discussion

1. What could Mrs. Kelly have done differently when teaching in the computer room? Would this have alleviated the problem all together?
2. Does Mrs. Kelly's task demonstrate a good use of technology in the classroom?
3. Do you think Mrs. Kelly has lost some of her hard-earned respect from her pupils? What will they be thinking of the quality of her teaching, and how might this impact their behavior in future lessons?
4. Do you think Shiloh should have informed her aunt of these potential consequences when sharing her lesson idea? Why or why not?
5. What responsibility does Mr. Hyslop and the senior team have in this issue? What strategies might they put in place to avoid a similar problem in the future? What support should they be offering Mrs. Kelly?
6. Many of Mrs. Kelly's pupils were clearly off task and a lot of the lesson time was wasted. What ramifications will this have on her next lesson? How will she deal with students at varying stage of the task?

CASE STUDY 5.6
CLASS VERSUS CLASSISM: THE INTERNET DIVIDE IN THE CLASSROOM

Standards 4.e, 5.b, and 5.f

Topic: Suburban high school. This case is about getting students acclimated to computers for the first time and how an introductory lesson in computer class is necessary due to student technology access even in this fast-paced, technology-driven world.

Eric knew when he entered the computer class that this would be an opportunity for him to learn more about computers than he ever had before. As a transfer student, he knew that his elementary school did not have the best equipment to teach students about the Internet, web coding, social media, or even email.

As a kid born in the 1990s, he couldn't even explain the difference between Facebook before it was just Harvard students to Facebook as it is today, primarily because he still had no idea how to effectively use a Facebook account. His lack of social media knowledge also included Twitter, Instagram, Tumblr, Snapchat, Pinterest, and more. But he was a fast learner and wanted to know more, so he joined the class.

His homeroom teacher had advised him against it after he admitted to her how little he knew of computers. But Eric felt this was unfair. It wasn't that he didn't want to know more about the web world. His family and his school simply just didn't have the funds to do so. Why should he be punished because of it? So here he was walking into the classroom of twenty-five, with five laptops on each round table. His grandmother had gifted with him a used smartphone, but he wasn't sure how to use it beyond email, the alarm, and making phone calls.

He sat down at a table by himself, watching a group of guys come into the classroom and flop down around his table speaking to each other but not him. He looked around the room and saw a room of guys and only one girl. He'd briefly heard during a Career Day forum, with a female web coder in attendance, at his last school how rare it was to find women versus men in the coder industry, but looking around this classroom made that more than apparent. However, in this case, even she appeared to know most of the guys in the room.

Being in a room of strangers didn't bother him so much as being in a class where he wasn't sure he'd be able to follow along. The teacher, also male, walked into the classroom and immediately told them to "reboot your computers, clear the cache and temporary Internet files to avoid clashing with whatever the other students programmed."

He looked around the classroom, wondering what in the world "cache" and "temporary Internet files" meant. Instead of following the directions, he sat in front of his laptop and watched the screensaver of triangles circle around until the rest of the room looked like they were done.

He looked down at a syllabus, with a calendar attached counting down all of the things that they'd learn in this course: social media marketing and demographics, Google Analytics versus Omniture, Understanding the Cloud, Mac and PC shortcuts, content management systems, basic troubleshooting, responsive web design, HTML coding, cascading style sheets basics, and a few other terms that were foreign to him.

"Hi class, my name is Mr. Frazier," a thirty-something man said at the front of the classroom. "Welcome to Computers 101. So you have your syllabus on your desk. We're going to run through a bunch of these topics, but I already know you guys probably know this stuff, so we'll move through this pretty quickly.

"But before we do, I want to get an idea of who knows what," Mr. Frazer continued. "I'm going to say all of the categories on this list, and you raise your hands to tell me what level you're at. For example, if you're a beginner at using the Cloud, raise your hand when I say 'Beginner—Cloud.' If intermediate, raise your hand then. If advanced, raise your hand for that. This'll give me an idea of what areas to focus on the most. I'm going to take a poll on it all. Deal?"

The class mumbled a few yeses or nodded their heads. Mr. Frazier started from top to bottom, running down the entire list. The closer he got to the end, the more Eric wanted to sink into his seat. He hadn't raised his hand once. Shouldn't these kinds of questions have been answered privately, such as a survey? Or maybe a test? Eric felt on the spot and wondered how many people at his table noticed he never moved his arms. Unfortunately for him, Mr. Frazier was also paying close attention to who was participating.

"Hey buddy, you sleep over there?" Mr. Frazier asked, looking in Eric's direction.

Eric looked behind him and then pointed to himself. "No, I'm not."

"Did you understand the directions I gave?" Mr. Frazier asked him.

"Yes," Eric responded.

"Well, what are you waiting for?" Mr. Frazier quipped. "Did you want me to call on you personally or something."

Eric shook his head no. He noticed a few pairs of eyes on him.

"OK, I see how this is going to go," Mr. Frazier sighed. "You must be an expert in all of them, huh? Listen, all freshmen have to take this class in order to advance to other courses."

Eric looked down at his hands. "No," he mumbled.

"Well, I sure hope you're at least a beginner on all of them," Mr. Frazier said, laughing. "Otherwise you're in the wrong classroom. Better get to Computer 001 instead of Computer 101 in that case."

Eric looked up, stunned at the joke. He didn't reply.

"Suit yourself, buddy," Mr. Frazier said, rubbing his hands together. "We've got work to do. Today we'll look at exploring demographics on social media: top bit.ly tweets, Facebook reaches and fans, Pinterest Analytics and repins, that kind of thing. Can you guys log into your accounts now so we can get started?"

Eric continued staring at his screen, wondering what in the world any of that meant.

"Hey, I've got a question," one of the students asked.

"Shoot," Mr. Frazier said.

"Why are we looking at Pinterest?" the student asked. "Isn't that kind of for girls? My sister calls it 'the site for sad girls.'"

Most of the class laughed along, minus the only girl in the class.

"Excuse you," she snipped. "I like Pinterest, and I'm not a sad girl."

"All right, all right," Mr. Frazier said. "Settle down. Sad Girl and Computer 001, you two partner up, and let's get class going. I shared a Google Doc with all of you already at the start of class. Open it up and respond to all of the questions. You should be able to get all of them done by the end of class."

The girl rolled her eyes and scooted her way over to Eric's desk with her laptop.

"That was kind of mean, huh?" Eric said to her.

"I'm used to it," she said. "Don't worry. These guys are harmless. I knew most of them in junior high. It's a boy's club in computer classes always. I'm sure you know that already. Let's get started, OK?"

Eric looked from her to his computer, wondering if he should start his computer or start his way out of the door instead. This was not a boy's club he knew anything about.

Instead of admitting that he wasn't quite sure what to do, he decided to try another alternative. "How about I watch you today?" he asked her. "We can prove to all of these guys that girls are experts, too. What do you think?"

The girl smiled. "Sounds like a plan. My name is Charlotte."

Eric introduced himself and then looked onto her computer to watch her get started, quietly observing what she was doing. As she typed out notes on the Google Doc app, he compared what she typed to what he saw on the screen. Eric smiled, realizing this may not be as difficult as he thought it was. At least once he signed up for these accounts.

"Hey, Sad Girl, you doing OK over there?" Mr. Frazier asked from across the room.

"Yeah, fine," Charlotte mumbled. "And my name is Charlotte."

"OK, Sad Girl, got it. Computer 001, are you going to fill in any of your answers, too? I can see her answers but your document is still blank."

Eric looked up confused.

"Yeah, that's the one downside of Google Docs," Charlotte told Eric. "Since it's updated in real time, teachers can see what we're doing the whole time."

Instead of asking what "real time" was, Eric asked Charlotte to help him figure out how to get to the document. He did have an email account set up but wasn't sure what to do past that.

"You seriously don't know how to get to the document?" Charlotte asked, staring at him quizzically.

"I don't," Eric said.

"I think you should tell Mr. Frazier that then. Otherwise he's going to think you're just messing around."

Eric knew it was inevitable. If he could tell his homeroom teacher, he should be able to tell Mr. Frazier, too. But before he could make his way to the front of the class to try to talk to him while the other students were distracted, Mr. Frazier had already made his way over.

"What are you doing?" he asked Eric.

"Nothing," Eric responded.

"I know," Mr. Frazier said. "Look, you can flirt with Sad Girl after class. Right now I need you to open that doc so we can get a move on."

"It's Charlotte," Charlotte repeated through clinched teeth.

"OK, OK, Charlotte," Mr. Frazier said. "Listen, I'm going to need you to go back to your seat. Otherwise Computer 001 won't get anything done."

Another student at the table laughed. "He called you Computer 001 like it's 007 or something."

The other students at the table laughed along. Eric decided at that very moment that he'd rather drop the class than be embarrassed any longer.

Questions for Discussion

1. Should Mr. Frazier have chosen an alternate way to measure the class level, such as a written poll or test?
2. Should Eric have taken his homeroom teacher's advice and not signed up for this class?
3. Are the types of subjects being taught in Computer 101 too advanced for this class or should these topics be common knowledge for students of this age? If so, what would be an alternate for students like Eric?
4. Should Mr. Frazier have put a stop to the comments about Pinterest although the site does have a higher demographic of female users? Would the student's comment be considered sexist?

5. Should Eric give the class a chance, utilizing the help of his student partner, or should the teacher be held solely accountable for what Eric learns?
6. What should be an alternate way for beginner computer students who don't have as much experience as others?

Selected Bibliography

Achieve. (2016). *Proficient vs. Prepared. Report.* Retrieved from: http://www.achieve.org/files/ProficiencyvsPrepared2.pdf.
Ball, D. L., & Cohen, D. K. (1996). Reform by the book: What is: Or might be: The role of curriculum materials in teacher learning and instructional reform? *Educational Researcher*, 25(9), 6–14.
Bambrick-Santoyo, P. (2012). *Leverage leadership: A practical guide to building exceptional schools.* Hoboken, NJ: John Wiley & Sons.
Barnes, C. R. (2011). Race to the top only benefits big government. *Journal of Law and Education*, 40(2), 393–402.
Bartlett, L., & Vavrus, F. (2014). Traversing the vertical case study: A methodological approach to studies of educational policy as practice. *Anthropology & Education Quarterly*, 45(2), 131–47.
Blase, J., & Blase, Jo. (2000). Effective instructional leadership: Teachers' perspective on how principals promote teaching and learning in schools. *Journal of Educational Administration*, 38(2), 130–41.
Blasé, J., & Kirby, P. C. (2009). *Bringing out the best in teachers: What effective principals do*, second edition. Thousand Oaks, CA: Corwin Press.
Boberg, J. E., & Bourgeois, S. J. (2016). The effects of integrated transformational leadership on achievement. *Journal of Educational Administration*, 54(3).
Bolman, L. G., & and Deal, T. E., (2013). *Reframing organizations: Artistry, choice, and leadership*, fifth edition. San Francisco, CA: Jossey-Bass.
Breidenstein, A., Fahey, K., Glickman, C., & Hensley, F. (2012). *Leading for powerful learning: A guide for instructional leaders.* New York: Teachers College Press.
Bright, N. H. (2011). Five habits of highly effective teachers. *School Administrator*, 68(9), 33–35.
Bryk, A., Harding, H., & Greenberg, S. (2012). Contextual influences on inquiries into effective teaching and their implications for improving student learning. *Harvard Educational Review*, 82(1), 83–106.
Bryk, A. S., Sebring, P. B., Allensworth, E., Easton, J. Q., & Luppescu, S. (2010). *Organizing schools for improvement: Lessons from Chicago.* Chicago: University of Chicago Press.
Burch, P., & Spillane, J. (2002). *Making sense of accountability pressures: Intermediary actors as interpreters of district instructional policy.* Evanston, IL: Northwestern University.
Christensen, R. (1981). *Teaching by the Case Method.* Cambridge: Harvard Business School Press.
Danielson, C. (2012). It's your evaluation – Collaborating to improve teacher practice. The *Education Digest*, 77(8), 22–27.

Selected Bibliography

Danielson, C. (2013). *The framework for teacher evaluation instrument*. Princeton, NJ: The Danielson Group.

Danielson, C., & McCrea, T. L. (2000). Teacher Evaluation: To Enhance Professional Practice. Alexandria, VA: *Association for Supervision and Curriculum Development*.

Darling-Hammond, L. (2000). (intro)

Darling-Hammond, L. (2013). *Getting teacher evaluation right: What really matters for effectiveness and improvement*. New York: Teachers College, Columbia University.

Darling-Hammond, L., Amrein-Beardsley, A., Haertel, E., & Rothstein, J. (2012). Evaluating teacher evaluation. *Phi Delta Kappan*, 93(6), 8–15.

Duffrin, E. (2011). What's the value in value-added? *District Administration*, 77(2), 46–49.

DuFour, R., & Marzano, R. (2011). *Leaders of learning: How district, school, and classroom leaders improve student achievement*. Bloomington, IN: Solution Tree Press.

Duke, D. (n.d.). *Keys to sustaining successful school turnaround*. Charlottesville, VA: Darden/Curry Partnership for Leaders in Education. Retrieved from: http://www.darden.edu/html/standard.aspx?menu_id=39&styleid=3&id=3215.

Durand, F. T., Lawson, H. A., Wilcox, K. C., & Schiller, K. S. (2015). The role of district office leaders in the adoption and implementation of the common core state standards in elementary schools. *Educational Administration Quarterly*, 52(1), 45–74.

Eckert, J. M., & Dabrowski, J. (2010). Should value-added measures be used for performance pay? *Phi Delta Kappan*, 9(8), 88–92.

Elder, C. H. (2004). *Dismissal doesn't have to be difficult: What every administrator and supervisor should know*. Lanham, MD: Rowman and Littlefield.

Eilers, L. H., & D'Amico, M. (2012). Essential leadership elements in implementing common core state standards. *Delta Kappa Gamma Bulletin*, 78(4), 46–50.

Engebritson, R. (2008). Courage to let bad teachers go. *School Administrator*, 65(8), 44–45. Retrieved from Education Research Complete database.

Evans, R. (1996). *The human side of school change: Reform, resistance, and the real-life problems of innovation*. San Francisco, CA: Jossey-Bass.

Fabry, D. L. (2010). Combing research-based effective teacher characteristics with effective instructional strategies to influence pedagogy. *Journal of Research in Innovative Teaching*, 3(1), 24–32.

Feeney, E. J. (2007). Quality feedback: The essential ingredient for teacher success. *Clearing House*, 80(4), 91–98.

Fenstermacher, G. D., & Richardson, V. (2005). On making determinations of quality in teaching. *Teachers College Record*, 107(1), 186–213.

Fink, S., & Markholt, A. (2011). *Leading for instructional improvement: How successful leaders develop teaching and learning expertise*, first edition. San Francisco, CA: Jossey-Bass.

Fink, S., & Resnick, L. B. (2001). Developing principals as instructional leaders. *Phi Delta Kappan*, 82(8), 598–606.

Fullan, M. (2014). *The Principal: Three keys to maximizing impact*. San Francisco, CA: Jossey-Bass.

Gerring, John. (2007). *Case study research: Principles and practices*. New York: Cambridge University Press.

Glanz, J. (2005). Action research as instructional supervision: Suggestions for principals. *NASSP Bulletin*, 89(643), 17–27.

Glaser, B. G. (1965). The constant comparative method of qualitative analysis. *Social Problems*, 12(4), 436–45.

Glickman, C. D., Gordon, S.P., & Ross-Gordon, J.M. (2010). *Supervision and instructional leadership: A developmental approach* (8th ed.). Boston, MA: Pearson.

Goldring, E., Cravens, X. C., Murphy, J., Porter, A. C., Elliott, S. N., & Carson, V. (2009). The evaluation of principals: What and how do states and urban districts assess leadership? *The Elementary School Journal*, 110(1), 19–39.

Griffin, L. (2013). Charlotte Danielson on teacher evaluation and quality. *School Administrator*, 70(1), 27–31. Retrieved from: http://www.aasa.org/content.aspx?id.

Hallinger, P. (1992). The evolving role of American principals: From managerial to instructional to transformational leaders. *Journal of Education Administration*, 30, 35–48.

Hallinger, P. (2003). Research on the practice of instructional and transformational leadership: retrospect and prospect. *Cambridge Journal of Education*, 33(3), 329–51.

Hallinger, P. (2008). A review of PIMRS studies of principal instructional leadership: assessment of progress over 25 years. Paper prepared for presentation at the annual meeting of the American Educational Research Association, New York.

Hallinger, P., & Heck, R. (1996). Reassessing the principal's role in school effectiveness. *Educational Administration Quarterly*, 32(1), 5–44.

Hallinger, P., & Heck, R. (1998). Exploring the principal's contribution to school effectiveness: 1980-1995. *School Effectiveness and School Improvement*, 9(2), 157–91.

Hallinger, P., & Leithwood, K (1998). Unseen forces: The impact of social culture on leadership. *Peabody Journal of Education*, 73(2), 126–51.

Hargreaves, A., & Fink, D. (2004). The seven principles of sustainable leadership. *Educational Leadership*, 61(7), 8–13.

Hargreaves, A., & Fullan, M. (2012). *Professional capital: Transforming teaching in every school*. New York: Teachers College Press.

Heifetz, R. A., and Linsky, M. (2002). *Leadership on the line: Staying alive through the dangers of leading*. Boston, MA: Harvard Business School Press.

Hozien, W. (2017). *SLLA Crash Course: Approaches to Success*. Lanham, MD: Rowman & Littlefield.

Kane, T. J. (2015). *Did the Common Core assessments cause the decline in NAEP scores?* Evidence Speaks: Series #13. Washington, DC: Brookings Institute. Retrieved from: http://www.brookings.edu/research/papers/2015/11/05-common-coreassessments-decline-in-naep-scores-kane.

Kaufman, J. H., Hamilton, L. S., Stecher, B. M., Naftel, S., Robbins, M., Thompson, L. E., Garber, C., Faxon-Mills, S., & Opfer, V. D. (2016). *What supports do teachers need to help students meet common core state standards for English language arts and literacy? Findings from the American Teacher, and American School Leader Panels*. Santa Monica, CA: RAND Corporation. Retrieved from: http://www.rand.org/pubs/research_reports/RR1374.html.

Lambert, L. (2003). *Leadership capacity for lasting school improvement*. Alexandria, VA: Association for Supervision and Curriculum Development.

Learning Forward. (2016.) *Meet the promise of content standards: The principal*. Oxford, OH: Learning Forward.

Leithwood, K. (1994). Leadership for school restructuring. *Educational Administration Quarterly*, 30(4), 498–518.

Leithwood, K., & Jantzi, D. (2008). Linking leadership to student learning: The contributions of leader efficacy. *Educational Administration Quarterly*, 44(4). Retrieved from http://journals.sagepub.com/doi/abs/10.1177/0013161X08321501.

Leithwood, K. A. & Riehl, C. (2003). What we know about school leadership. *National College for School Leadership*, http://www.ncsl.org.uk/mediastore/irnage2/randdleithwood-successful-leadership.pdf.

Leithwood, K., Louis, K. S., Anderson, S., & Wahlstrom, K. (2004). *How leadership influences student learning*. New York: Wallace Foundation.

Leonhart, D. (2010, Sept. 1). When does holding teachers accountable go too far? *The New York Times*. Retrieved from: http://www.nytimes.com/2010/09/05/magazine/05FOB-wwln-t.html.

Levin, J., & Nolan, J. F. (2013). *Principles of classroom management: A professional decision-making model*. London, England: Pearson Higher Education.

Louis, K., Dretzke, B., & Wahlstrom, K. (2010). How does leadership affect student achievement? Results from a national US survey. *School Effectiveness and School Improvement*, 21(3), 315–36.

Loveless, T. (2016). *2016 Brown Center report on American education: How well are American students learning?* Washington, DC: Brookings Institute.

Mangiante, E. (2011). Teachers matter: Measures of teacher effectiveness in low-income minority schools. *Educational Assessment, Evaluation & Accountability*, 23(1).

Marks, H., & Printy, S. (2003). Principal leadership and school performance: An integration of transformational and instructional leadership. *Educational Administration Quarterly*, 39(3), 370–97.

Marks, H., & Nance, J. (2007). Contexts of accountability under systemic reform: Implications for principal influence on instruction and supervision. *Educational Administration Quarterly*, 43(1), 3–37.

Marshall, K. (2006). Teacher evaluation rubrics: The why and the how. *Phi Delta Kappan*, September/October 2006.

Marshall, K. (2009). *Rethinking teacher supervision and evaluation: How to work smart, build collaboration, and close the achievement gap*. San Francisco, CA: Jossey-Bass.

Marshall, K. (2014a). *Evaluation rubrics*. Retrieved from: http://www.marshallmemo.com/articles/Teacher%20rubrics%20Jan%202014.pdf.

Marshall, K. (2014b). How the Danielson rubric could be more effective for city teachers and principals. *Chalkbeat*. Retrieved from: http://www.chalkbeat.org/posts/ny/2014/04/11/how-the-danielson-rubric-could-be-more-effective-for-new-york-city-teachers/#.V0N_Z5MrI_V.

Marzano, R. (2003). *What works in schools: Translating research into action*. Alexandria, VA: Association for Supervision and Curriculum Development.

Marzano, R. J. (2006). *Classroom assessment and grading that works*. Alexandria, VA: Association for Supervision and Curriculum Development.

Marzano, R. J. (2013a). *Marzano causal teacher evaluation*. Retrieved from: http://www.marzanocenter.com/Teacher-Evaluation/.

Marzano, R. J. (2013b). *The Marzano teacher evaluation model*. Englewood, CO: Marzano Research Laboratory.

Marzano, R. J., & Toth, M.D. (2013). *Teacher evaluation that makes a difference*. Alexandria, VA: Association for Supervision and Curriculum Development.

Marzano, R., Frontier, T., & Livingston, D. (2011). *Effective supervision: Supporting the art and science of teaching*. Alexandria, VA: Association for Supervision and Curriculum Development.

Marzano, R. J., Waters, T., & McNulty, B. A. (2005). *School leadership that works: From research to results*. Alexandria, VA: Association for Supervision and Curriculum Development.

McGreal, T. L. (1983). *Successful teacher evaluation*. Alexandria, VA: Association for Supervision and Curriculum Development.

Miles, M. B., & Huberman, A. M. (1994). Qualitative data analysis: An expanded sourcebook. New York: Sage.

Milner, H. R. (2013). *Policy reforms and de-professionalization of teaching*. Boulder, CO: National Education Policy Center. Retrieved from: http://nepc.colorado.edu/publication/policy.

Murphy, J. (2007). Restructuring through learning-focused leadership. In H. Walberg (Ed.), *Handbook on restructuring and substantial school improvement* (pp. 71–84). Lincoln, IL: Center on Innovation and Improvement.

National Association of Elementary School Principals. (2008). *Leading learning communities: Standards for what principals should know and be able to do*. Retrieved from: https://www.naesp.org/resources/1/Pdfs/LLC2-ES.pdf.

National Policy Board for Educational Administration. (2015). *Professional standards for educational leaders 2015*. Reston, VA: Author.

Northouse, P. G. (2007). *Leadership: Theory and practice*. Thousand Oaks, CA: Sage Publications, Inc.

Peterson, P. E., Barrows, S., & Gift, T. (2016). *After common core, states set rigorous standards. Education Next*, 16(3).

Reeves, D. B. (2006). *The learning leader: How to focus school improvements for better results*. Alexandria, VA: Association for Supervision and Curriculum Development.

Robbins, P., & Alvy, H. (2004). *The new principals fieldbook: Strategies for success*. Alexandria, VA: Association for Supervision and Curriculum Development.

Schmoker, M. (2006). *Results now: How we can achieve unprecedented improvements in teaching and learning*. Alexandria, VA: Association for Supervision and Curriculum Development.

Schweitzer, Karen, (2014). How to write case study analysis? *Harvard Business Review*. Retrieved from: http://businessmajors.about.com/od/casestudies/ht/HowToCaseStudy.htm.

Seed, A. H. (2008). Redirecting the teaching profession in the wake of a nation at risk and NCLB. *Phi Delta Kappan*, 89(8), 586–89.

Sergiovanni, T. J. (2001). *Leadership: What's in it for schools?* New York, NY: Routledge Falmer.

Shulman, L. S. (1983) Autonomy and obligation: The remote control of teaching. In Shulman, L.S., & Sykes G. (Eds.), *Handbook of teaching and policy* (pp. 484–504). New York: Longman.

Stigler, J. W., & Hiebert, J. (1998). Teaching is a cultural activity. *American Educator*, 22(4), 4–11.

Stosich, E. L. (2015). Learning to teach to the common core state standards: examining the role of teachers' collaboration, principals' leadership, and professional development. Doctoral dissertation, Harvard Graduate School of Education. Retreived from http://dash.harvard.edu/handle/1/14121780.

Stronge, J. (1991). The dynamics of effective performance evaluation systems in education: Conceptual, human relations, and technical domains. *Journal of Personnel Evaluation in Education*, 5, 77–83.

Stronge, J. (2013). Teacher effectiveness performance evaluation system. Retrieved from: http://www.mcvea.org/extras/StrongeBook.pdf.

Tucker, P. D. & Stronge, J. H. (2005). *Linking teacher evaluation and student learning*. Alexandria, VA: Association for Supervision and Curriculum Development.

U.S. Department of Education. (2010). *A blueprint for reform: The reauthorization of the Elementary and Secondary Education Act*. Arlington, VA: U.S. Department of Education. Retrieved from: http://www2.ed.gov/policy/elsec/leg/blueprint/.

Wallace Foundation. (2012.) *The school principal as leader: Guiding schools to better teaching and learning*. New York: Wallace Foundation.

Watson, S., Miller, T., Davis, L., & Carter, P. (2010). Teachers' perceptions of the effective teacher. *Research in the Schools*, 17(2), 11–22.

About the Author

Dr. Wafa Hozien's professional background includes over twenty years' work as a high school history teacher and a school administrator. Dr. Hozien has designed and delivered training for school districts, universities, and leadership academies throughout the United States and internationally. She specializes in combining research-based strategies and practical applications, working with school administrators, teacher leaders, and school districts to adopt innovative strategies for their locations. Specifically, the incorporation of issues related to culture, ethnicity, race, and religion in the education process are valued by Dr. Hozien as integral and important.

Dr. Hozien has published numerous articles and publications on diversity issues in education. To help reduce inequities in education, Dr. Hozien makes herself available by educating through interactive workshops at schools, community organizations, and campus lectures on cultural competency and social justice. She has been researching the experiences of adolescent minority female public schooling experiences. In the multicultural education context, she has published and presented at workshops and conferences on minority student experiences.

Presently, she is an assistant professor of educational leadership at Central Michigan University where she teaches graduate students in the principal/superintendent doctoral preparation programs. Nondiscrimination and equality are key principles that Dr. Hozien applies to education in all of her courses.

Dr. Hozien appreciates constructive feedback and gaining insight as to best practices and ways to improve this book. If you find that this book is missing something or you have suggestions for improvement, then kindly contact the author via email; Dr. Hozien can be reached at whozien@gmail.com.

Dr. Hozien's most recent book is entitled *SLLA Crash Course: Approaches for Success* (Rowman & Littlefield, 2017).

www.ingramcontent.com/pod-product-compliance
Lightning Source LLC
Chambersburg PA
CBHW020750230426
43665CB00009B/554